ESSENTIAL INTERVIEWING SKILLS

FOR THE HELPING PROFESSIONS

Essential Interviewing Skills for the Helping Professions

A SOCIAL JUSTICE AND WELLNESS APPROACH

Nicole Nicotera, PhD, LICSW
UNIVERSITY OF DENVER, GRADUATE SCHOOL OF SOCIAL WORK

OXFORD
UNIVERSITY PRESS

Oxford University Press is a department of the University of Oxford. It furthers
the University's objective of excellence in research, scholarship, and education
by publishing worldwide. Oxford is a registered trade mark of Oxford University
Press in the UK and certain other countries.

Published in the United States of America by Oxford University Press
198 Madison Avenue, New York, NY 10016, United States of America.

© Oxford University Press 2018

CIP data is on file at the Library of Congress
ISBN 978-0-19-087687-6

Contents

Preface

Essential Interviewing Skills for the Helping Professions: A Social Justice and Wellness Approach reaches beyond most other books on essential skills for clinical interviewing with its emphasis on social justice, attention to the role of microaggressions in clinical practice, and the upmost importance of wellness as integral to longevity in the helping professions. Each chapter addresses interviewing skills that are foundational to the helping professions from mental health to physical health, includes detailed exercises for practicing those skills, attends to social justice, and engages the practitioner with wellness opportunities.

Clinical interviewing skills are the foundation of clinical practice in any of the helping professions, from clinical social work to nursing and doctoring to physical therapy and educational psychology. The most skilled clinical interviewers may appear to be engaged in a simple conversation with a client or patient, thereby making the process appear effortless. However, any clinical interviewer will explain that what appears effortless on the surface is actually guided by a foundation of knowledge pertinent to their profession and intensive practice in listening and responding with integrity and intention. The skilled interviewer simultaneously listens while deciphering what the client is saying and using the appropriate clinical interviewing skill to engage the client in telling his or her story with as much ease as feasible.

Regardless of how expert a clinical interviewer becomes, all began where you are today, as students in the foundational course work of their profession or as a newly trained graduate embarking on a first positon in their field of practice. The only way to gain the clinical interviewing skills you need to succeed with clients and/or patients is to practice, practice, and practice more. It requires being open to feeling a bit odd recording yourself in role-played scenarios and in real client interactions, when you have the client's permission. Gaining skills also requires that you share these recordings with professors, clinical supervisors, and colleagues with an open attitude of learning from constructive feedback. It also requires a commitment to life-long learning: Even after years of clinical interviewing practice, helping professionals spend their days with individuals who are most likely at their worst moments or they would not be seeking help, making the clinical interview a complex and ever-changing process.

The clinical interviewing process requires moment-by-moment choices, such as whether to use silence, empathy, or to challenge incongruous behavior. Sometimes clients' stories are fraught with trauma, other times their stories are bound within generations of substance addiction or family violence, and other clinical stories present personal and social obstacles that arise from years of oppression at the hands of prejudice and discrimination. Some of the more complicated stories are a combination of all of these aspects. Therefore, essential skills for clinical interviewing goes beyond the basic ideas of choosing when to use an open question or to reflect emotions but also covers how to integrate social justice and knowledge of power, privilege, and oppression into the interviewing arena. Essential interviewing skills require the practitioner to not only purposefully listen to the client's story but also to be self-aware and to be willing to acknowledge mistakes and learn from them. The work of the clinical interviewer is a continuous challenge of balancing listening, responding, action, and self-awareness, and it requires skills for wellness.

Chapter 1 engages the reader in listening with the whole heart and mind. It focuses on the basic skills for building rapport with clients and patients and emphasizes tone of voice, facial expressions, and body language. Readers engage in practice of skills for attending to the whole person with person-centered values, responding to microaggressions, and a first wellness exercise. This chapter also includes resources for creating deliverables for online teaching and learning.

Chapter 2 includes skills for ethical interviewing, such how to obtain informed consent, explain confidentiality, and practice within one's competence. Readers are challenged to consider the ethics of boundaries, power, and social justice; practice the skill of appropriate self-disclosure; apply the skills with a social justice approach; and complete a wellness activity.

In Chapter 3, readers are introduced to the skills necessary for obtaining a client's initial story such as the use of open and closed questions and the related topic of how the practitioner as "questioner" equates to power from the very start of the clinical relationship. Readers are also engaged in learning and practicing paraphrasing and summarizing as well as skills for wellness and social justice practice.

Chapter 4 covers skills that are foundational to gaining a deeper view on the client's story by uncovering and attending to emotions, assisting clients in discovering the meanings they place on their story and experiences, and challenging incongruous actions. The chapter places these skills in the context of the person-centered approach, examining the core elements of that approach from a social justice framework. The chapter presents the breath as a soothing wellness activity.

Chapter 5 covers skills related to putting the client's story into context and setting goals. The skills needed to apply the eco-map tool to gain a full picture of the client's concerns and the players within those concerns are covered. Attention is paid to learning how oppressive experiences can be included in the eco-map. Readers are challenged to integrate the interviewing skills from the previous chapters for this purpose as well as to assess client readiness for change and develop client-driven goals. The wellness activity combines the body and mind as readers engage in a walking meditation.

Chapter 6 engages readers in applying beginning skills for intervention such as solution-focused elements (e.g., scaling questions, exception questions, and the miracle question) and skills for applying the empty chair for internal dialogues and external dialogues, which is especially useful for clients confronting experiences of microaggressions. Readers learn a wellness strategy, the 3-minute breathing space, which was developed for mindfulness-based cognitive therapy by Mark Williams and his colleagues at Oxford University.

Chapter 7 concludes the book with the skills required for evaluating the helping relationship and for closure. Readers apply the skills required for closing a single session as well as the skills for closing an entire helping relationship. Readers also engage with evaluating their own skills on a session-by-session basis, including social justice, power, and the potential presence of microaggressions during the session and how to follow up. An evidence-based wellness activity on cultivating gratitude closes the chapter.

Acknowledgments

IT IS A joy and honor to work with David Follmer and Oxford University Press to write *Essential Interviewing Skills for the Helping Professions: A Social Justice and Wellness Approach.* I want to acknowledge my teachers and clinical supervisors, who pressed me to gain the skills and knowledge for astute clinical social work practice. I am also indebted to the teachers who challenged me to integrate a social justice framework into every endeavor, from clinical practice to conducting research. I also want to thank the numerous students I have taught in my clinical interviewing skills course; I learn more and more about clinical skills every time I teach the content and exchange ideas with them. Finally, but certainly not least, I want to thank my spouse, Ellen Winiarczyk, for her support and patience.

Author Biography

PROFESSOR NICOTERA is a social work educator and coordinator of the clinical skills training and the mind–body courses for the Master of Social Work program at the University of Denver Graduate School of Social Work, where she also teaches mixed-methods research for the PhD program. She is also trained in the use of experiential therapies (low and portable ropes courses) with youth, family–youth groups, and couples. Her research and scholarship focus on promoting health and well-being across the life span; civic engagement and mindfulness practices as pathways to well-being; measuring civic development and civic engagement; interventions to enhance civic leadership and positive youth development; the role of risk, protection, and resilience in health; and the issues of unearned privilege and oppression in social work practice, education, and research. She is an active community-engaged scholar and collaborates with community agencies to conduct research on their programs and to help them use the results of that research to create stronger programs.

And now here is my secret, a very simple secret: It is only with the heart that one can see rightly; what is essential is invisible to the eye.

—ANTOINE DE SAINT-EXUPÉRY, *The Little Prince*

1

Skills for Building Rapport

LISTENING IS THE primary skill required for any clinical helping professional, regardless of whether the individual practices social work, medicine, nursing, counseling, psychology, or physical therapy, to name a few. Those of us who work in the helping professionals must gain skills for listening to more than the words a client uses to tell his or her story because words have many meanings and words do not communicate the entirety of a client's experience. Therefore, how we listen and what we listen for are important.

LISTENING WITH YOUR WHOLE HEART, MIND, AND BODY

Helping professionals listen not only for words but also for tone of voice. We use tone of voice in our daily lives to express ourselves, though we are not always aware of it or how it sounds to others. We use tone to express joy when we greet someone we care about or to express urgency or danger in order to stop someone from walking out in front of a car. However, tone of voice can also be more subtle and difficult to detect. Helping professionals need to become keenly aware of tone of voice even to the point of noting a client's intake of breath, which may signal he or she is about to speak. We can use silence to give the client room to speak or check in, perhaps asking, "Were you about to say something?" As clinicians, we need to be able to hear how our own tone sounds as well as the client's tone of voice.

It is fairly safe to interpret the tone of voice that warns you not to cross the street when a car is coming or the tone of joy you hear in a loved one's voice when he or she greets you. However, in professional clinical practice, we cannot assume we know the meaning associated with a client's tone of voice because our understanding of tone is culturally and linguistically bound. It is important to refrain from assuming what tone of voice means, even when you and the client share a similar culture and language.

In addition to listening for tone of voice, clinicians must also be adept at observing facial expressions and body language. Similar to tone of voice, we use facial expressions and body language in our daily lives, and we are often unaware of how we appear to others. Facial expressions and body language can be explicit, such as throwing one's arms in the air, or they can be subtle, such as the blink of an eye and a lowering of a gaze. Regardless of how obvious or subtle, the clinician should not assume he or she knows what gestures or facial expressions convey.

In sum, observing facial expressions and body language, and listening for tone of voice are called *attending skills*. The key to this set of interviewing skills is to remember that all listening and observation are culturally bound. That is, what you suppose a client means by tone of voice, gestures, or facial expressions is based on what you learned in your family, the first or home language you learned growing up, and social-cultural norms. Attending skills only alert you to these elements of what a client is telling you and must be followed up with interview skills such as effective questions, paraphrases, reflections of feeling, and eliciting of meaning, all of which are covered in subsequent chapters. The challenge for you just now is to practice the skills of listening for tone of voice and observing facial expressions and body language.

Skill Practice—Tone of Voice

- Pair up with a colleague or classmate.
- Take turns being the listener and the speaker.
- When you are the speaker, take about 5 minutes to respond to the following prompt: "Tell me about a favorite place, real or imagined."
- When you are the listener, *close your eyes for the entire time* and simply listen without asking questions or making comments.
- When you are listening, take note of how you are affected by your colleague's tone of voice. Can you hear any emotion(s) in the tone of voice? What does the tone of voice tell you about your colleague's favorite place?
- After each of you has played both listener and the speaker, (1) each person should share what you heard in your colleague's tone of voice and then (2) discuss what it was like to listen with eyes closed compared to your typical listening with eyes open.

- View the following media clips, which present exaggerated examples of facial expression and body language.
- Discuss each media clip with one or more classmates or colleagues: What did you learn about the power of facial expressions? What did you learn about the power of body language? What did you learn about tone of voice? How will you apply these in clinical interviewing?

Media Clip 1: Big bang theory on body language: https://www.youtube.com/watch?v=vicuZSoChYQ

Media Clip 2: The importance of nonverbal cues as told by friends: https://www.youtube.com/watch?v=OvEci5Bjgd4

- View the following media clip with your device on mute. The interview in and of itself has relevance for you as a clinical social worker, and this will be covered in a subsequent section of this chapter. So for now focus on watching it without the sound to practice the skills of observing facial expressions and body language.
- As you watch the interview, consider the following questions: What do their respective facial expressions communicate about how each of them feels about the topic? What about their facial expressions suggests how they are feeling in the moment itself? Identify moments of body language for each of them. What does it suggest about their rapport with each other?

Media Clip 3: Oprah Winfrey interviewing Dr. Brene Brown, PhD, a social work researcher who studies and writes about vulnerability: https://www.youtube.com/watch?v=RKVoBWSPfOw

MINDFUL USE OF SELF FOR ASTUTE LISTENING SKILLS

Attending skills are the primary building blocks of establishing rapport and beginning to earn the trust of a client. However, the skill of listening extends beyond these basics. Listening also occurs from and within the mind. What ideas and thoughts does the client's story call up in you? Does the story remind you of a personal experience, another client, a news story you heard on your way to work? The skill of listening with the mind is being aware of the ideas and thoughts that come to you when the client is telling his or her story so you can remain on target and stay in tune with the client's unique story.

In addition to listening with the mind, practitioners must also learn to listen with their body. This means being aware of how you react physically to a client's story. While you are listening, do you notice that your stomach hurts? Do you notice that your jaw or your fists are clenched? Are you tapping your finger or swinging your foot back and forth over and over again? Do you notice you are holding your breath? Do you feel sleepy or alert? These are some of the ways that your body may react to a client's story.

Listening with the heart or awareness of your emotional reactions to a client's story is the third aspect of mindful use of the self for listening. It involves posing and then answering the following types of questions to yourself as you listen to a client: What feelings come up as you listen to client stories? Do you find yourself feeling bored, anxious, sad, happy, resentful, angry, or peaceful? The capacity for this kind of listening requires you to have a strong feeling vocabulary and insight into your own emotions. This takes practice because many of us have not been schooled in tuning into our feelings. We are seldom taught how to build the capacity for identifying a wide range of feeling states in ourselves or others.

This skill of listening with the heart is called emotional intelligence (Goleman, 1998). Goleman (1998) describes a number of competencies related to emotional intelligence and defines it as "the capacity for recognizing our own feelings and those of others, for motivating ourselves, and for managing emotions well in ourselves and in our relationships" (p. 317). Listening with the heart involves the first and third aspects of that definition, recognizing your own emotions and those of your client as well as being able to regulate your feelings in the face of client stories. Emotional intelligence is a learned capacity, so the more you practice it, the better you can become at using it to serve your clients well and for your own emotional health.

Skill Practice—Listening With the Mind, Body, and Heart

Work with two or three classmates or colleagues for this exercise. First, each of you will follow the steps without telling each other your reactions. After each of you has completed all the steps, then share your reactions and discuss what may have caused them to be similar and different from each other. How might your unique backgrounds have led you to have different reactions? What do you have in common that may have created similar reactions?

- Read the following excerpt from an initial clinical session with a cisgender[1] female client and a cisgender male clinician in which the client describes her marriage (McKenzie, 2011, pp. 89–90; McKenzie & Nicotera, in press).

---

[1] *Cisgender* is a term that refers to individuals whose gender identity aligns with the biological sex they were assigned at birth.

- Be prepared to notice and make notes on what occurs in your mind as you read the excerpt. Note what the story makes you think about, such as relationships in general, heterosexual relationships specifically. What thoughts do you have about the client? What thoughts do you have about her husband? What thoughts do you have about the clinician?
- Be prepared to notice and make notes about what happens in your body as you read the excerpt. Are you relaxed? Do you feel any muscles tensing?
- Be prepared to pose and answer the following questions: What feelings come up as you read this client interview? For example, do you find yourself feeling bored, anxious, sad, happy, resentful, angry, peaceful, or some other feelings? Have a feeling chart on hand to assist with your emotional vocabulary. Feeling charts are readily available online and can be found by typing the words "feeling chart" into your Web browser.

DENISE: I don't think you could call it a marriage, let alone a relationship.

CLINICAL INTERVIEWER: Why do you say that?

DENISE: Well, he's barely involved with me. Oh yeah, he wants to have sex, but other than that, he is literally not there for me. Even in sex it's all about him.

CLINICAL INTERVIEWER: So, it sounds like he doesn't interact much with you. How long has this been going on?

DENISE: It seems like forever.

CLINICAL INTERVIEWER: How long have the two of you been married?

DENISE: Almost 10 years now. I guess things started to change after about 3 or 4 years.

CLINICAL INTERVIEWER: And prior to that time, how was he?

DENISE: He was OK, I guess. We seemed to share in the household activities, he used to sit and talk with me, and our lovemaking really seemed like love. But then it all started to change.

CLINICAL INTERVIEWER: How so?

DENISE: Like I said before, he just started getting more selfish and distant.

CLINICAL INTERVIEWER: To help me understand better, Denise, could you talk a little bit about how the two of you dealt with these changes?

DENISE: I tried to explain to him that he was acting different, and that I really needed and wanted him more involved with me and our home.

CLINICAL INTERVIEWER: And how did he respond?

DENISE: You know, like all men. He just couldn't see it and wasn't willing to try and change anything.

CLINICAL INTERVIEWER: That must have been very frustrating.

DENISE: How would you know, you're a man just like all the rest.

CLINICAL INTERVIEWER: I'm not sure I understand what you mean, Denise, when you say I'm a man just like all the rest?

DENISE: You're all just concerned about yourselves. You know, you just want us to cook, clean, get the groceries, have sex when you want, you know.

CLINICAL INTERVIEWER: How do you know that I am that kind of man?

DENISE: You're all the same.

MICROAGGRESSIONS

The capacity to work across multicultural and social identity differences is of major importance for building rapport with clients. Practitioners must become skilled in recognizing how their unintended words, gestures, and facial expressions can constitute microaggressions toward stereotyped groups based on race-ethnicity, sexual orientation, gender identity, disability, gender, religion, social class, and age, among others (Sue, 2007, 2010a, 2010b). Microaggressions are different from direct and targeted comments that tend to be delivered for the intended purpose of harming or shaming a targeted person, such as a racist or homophobic comment. Microaggressions are subtle, typically unintended, and can take the form of a comment, gesture, or tone of voice that suggests, for example, that a person of color or other stereotyped person does not belong, is a rarity when successful, is a criminal suspect, or is overreacting to experiences of racismio, to name a few (Sue, 2007; see also https://www.youtube.com/watch?v=9OnsMO19uw4).

It is important to point out the element of social power and privilege in microaggressions. For example, in the clinical interview example in the previous section, the client, Denise, tells the clinician that she feels like "men are all alike." This *does not* constitute a microaggression, even if it makes the male clinician uncomfortable, because men are not a targeted group. Similarly, if a person of color is frustrated about hearing yet another racist microaggression and comments that all White people are the same, it may make some White people uncomfortable, but it does not make them oppressed or constitute a microaggression. This is an important distinction in the process of working toward recognizing and unlearning microaggressions.

Although typically unintended, microaggressions in general and in clinical practice specifically, disrupt rapport and trust building. The unaware practitioner may find himself wondering why a client never returned after the first session or why it seems so difficult to build trust with a client, when in fact he may have unwittingly denigrated a client whose culture, religion, or other social identity is targeted by stereotyped assumptions and negative comments. The social emotional impact of microaggressions on the health of targeted groups contributes to problems such as depression and anxiety (Sue, 2007). Microaggressions impact a targeted individual's "performance in a multitude of settings by sapping the psychic and spiritual energy of recipients and by creating inequities" (Sue, 2007, p. 272).

Fortunately, practitioners who are willing to listen and learn without defensiveness can become aware of microaggressions in everyday life and in their own thoughts, words, and gestures and address them with behavior change and sincere apologies. In fact, some helping professions, such as social work, adhere to values and ethics that prescribe the need for uncovering and learning microaggressive actions and speaking out against this kind of injustice. Uncovering and unlearning microaggressions can be painful work as individuals realize that they have been unwittingly denigrating toward clients and others in their lives. However, this is a small cost to pay for developing stronger and more meaningful relationships with clients. Clients let us into their hearts and minds and "being privy to the innermost details of their . . . lives and deepest vulnerabilities requires levels of care, compassion, and empathy that only certain people are capable of delivering every day, over the course of their entire career" (Maskell, 2016, p. 14). Uncovering and unlearning microaggressions is part of becoming one of the "certain people" who is capable of serving clients with their whole hearts and minds over the course of a career. When you are willing to be vulnerable with the client by acknowledging and apologizing for missteps such as microaggressions, you open the door to a greater level of rapport with clients.

Skill Practice—Listening for and Responding to Microaggressions

- Read the following excerpt from a clinical session in which a cisgender, 60- year-old, male client describes some workplace concerns to a cisgender, 50-year-old female clinician (McKenzie, 2011; McKenzie & Nicotera, in press).
- Then discuss the interview with a small group of classmates or colleagues and address the following questions: Are there any microaggressions occurring in this interview? If yes, makes you think this? If no, what makes you think this? If there are microaggressions in this interview, which person(s) in the story is responsible for them? If there are microaggressions in this interview, what should be done about them, and who should respond and how?

FRANK: I had been working at this fairly large advertising firm for over 30 years. I started right out of college and was doing very well. I did so well on my team that I was given a series of promotions, and over the last 5 years or so I was in charge of my department, with a lot of responsibility. I supervised about 15 people directly, and many of them were supervisors under me who had people that reported to them. Everything seemed to be going great until my new boss demoted me.

INTERVIEWER: Sounds like this was a big surprise.

FRANK: Kind of . . . I have been having trouble with my boss for a while, and I think it has come to a head.

INTERVIEWER: Tell me more about that.

FRANK: I have known her for a long time. She has been with the company for about 15 years. Until recently I have not worked directly under her. When I interviewed with her for promotion several years ago, the first thing she said to me was "So . . . you have been here twice as long as me, you must want my job?" I didn't know what to say, but her statement really caught me off guard and made me think she was threatened by me.

INTERVIEWER: Yeah, that does sound that way.

FRANK: Ever since I got the promotion, she has been very difficult to work with . . .

INTERVIEWER: In what way?

FRANK: It's kind of hard to describe exactly. She did not meet with me on a regular basis except to direct me to take on some type of task. She never asked my opinion about my area, which is a huge portion of the company. She cut me off in conversations, and just didn't seem interested in anything I have to say.

INTERVIEWER: So let me see if I understand. You had been doing well at work, so well that you had gotten promoted to a fairly high position with a good deal of responsibility, but now your immediate supervisor seemed to be opposed to you, or perhaps even threatened?

FRANK: Yeah, does that sound crazy?

INTERVIEWER: Well, from how you describe things, it sounds like this is a huge surprise, very unexpected, and troublesome. At the same time, you must be getting close to retirement. I wonder if your boss is planning for the future and demoted you so you could train a younger person for the job before the agency loses your expertise.

FRANK: Well, there are a couple of other strange interactions I have had with her that I think you should know about.

INTERVIEWER: OK.

FRANK: The two of us were headed to a meeting a while ago, and she told me that one of the people on my team mentioned that they thought it might be helpful if she was a little more encouraging. My boss said, "Doesn't that person know I don't care about people!" She also said in a small meeting of supervisors like me, "You know the problem with this country? Old people who can't keep pace with the changes!"

INTERVIEWER: This sounds like a complicated situation.

PERSON-CENTERED VALUES

Building rapport is a continual process in any clinical relationship; it is a journey and not an end. Each time you meet with a client you have the opportunity to earn his or her trust and build rapport. Building rapport and earning trust involve the clinician's willingness to work toward demonstrating genuineness, unconditional positive regard, and empathy (Rogers, 1957, 2007) with each client. These three elements of clinical practice arise from Carl Rogers's person-centered approach to counseling and require continual growth and willingness to be vulnerable on the part of the clinician.

Genuineness refers to the clinician's capacity to be her true self in relationship with the client (Rogers, 1957, 2007) in a context of healthy self-awareness and boundaries. For example, Rogers points out that genuineness does not mean always sharing exactly what is on your mind with a client, but it includes the practitioner's awareness of the feelings and/or thoughts a client calls up in him. For example, a practitioner may become aware that he feels threatened by a client or that his own personal problems are clouding his capacity to listen fully to the client (Rogers, 1957, 2007). Genuineness in this context means that the practitioner admits to himself that he has these feelings and thoughts and seeks out supervision or consultation with a trusted colleague. Genuineness also includes sharing reactions to a client's story while maintaining appropriate and healthy boundaries (Rogers, 1957, 2007). For example, a client's personal story of emotional pain may bring a tear to the practitioner's eye and the genuine practitioner will not try to hide this teardrop, but instead communicate the tear as an expression of empathy for the client. Simultaneously, genuineness means that the practitioner is aware of the difference between a teardrop in empathy versus a deluge of tears, suggesting that the tears are not so much empathy for the client, but instead an indication of the practitioner's own unresolved painful experience. In the latter example, the practitioner does indeed to need to rein in her tears and seek supervision and her own therapy to address the unresolved issue.

Unconditional positive regard refers to the practitioner's caring and "warm acceptance of each aspect of the client's experience as being part of that client" (Rogers, 2007, p. 243). The practitioner who expresses unconditional positive regard for clients demonstrates the capacity to accept the client as he is and to see strengths or goodness in the client irrespective of whether his story involves him as a perpetrator of violence such as murder, child abuse, domestic violence, or some form of self-harm such as cutting, addiction, or a suicidal attempt (Rogers, 1957, 2007). This acceptance and search for strengths does not mean that the practitioner condone a client's violent acts or self-harming behaviors. Instead, it means seeing some strength in the client for contending with lived experiences and related internal pain and suffering that lead to perpetration of violence against others or the self. Unconditional positive regard in conjunction with genuineness means that the clinician can confront a client as responsible for actions that harm others or himself (genuineness) while simultaneously finding and acknowledging a client's strengths (unconditional positive regard).

Rogers (1957, 2007) defined empathy as the practitioner's capacity "to sense the client's anger, fear, or confusion as if it were [the practitioner's] own, yet without getting bound up in it" [as if it were the practitioner's anger, fear, or confusion] (p. 243). The same would be true for sensing a client's pleasant emotions such as joy, happiness, or peacefulness—that is, sensing the client's feelings without owning them or taking up the emotional space that the client needs to express them. This definition of empathy communicates the clear need for healthy boundaries and self-awareness on the part of the practitioner, which is inherent in Rogers's description of genuineness.

Skill Practice—Listening With Person-Centered Values

- Read the following case example about Joan, a 30-year-old White woman who is a single mother. As you read it, be aware of and makes notes for yourself on what the case circumstances call up in you: What feelings arise? What thoughts arise? If you find yourself taking sides with Joan or one of her children, become aware of the reasons you take sides with that person.
- Now imagine that you are the child and family therapist who is working with Joan and her children as she works toward Child Protective Services requirements for reunification with Jim. How will you use person-centered values of genuineness, unconditional positive regard, and empathy to build rapport with Joan?

Joan is a White, 30-year-old, single mother of four children, each of whom has a different father. Joan gave birth to her first child when she was 15 years old. She has used drugs off and on for the past year, saying that they help her cope with her 15-year-old daughter, Melody, who she says *"gets on her last nerve."* Joan maintains several part-time jobs and uses public assistance to support her family. Her 5-year-old son, Jim, was recently removed from her home under suspicion of neglect and physical abuse. Joan claims that she does not hurt Jim. She says, "I am a good parent and punish Jim so he will be respectful of women when he grows up." However, Jim was removed by Child Protective Services after he told his teacher that his mom slaps him and pushes him around and then locks him in his room without dinner. Joan says she loves and misses Jim and wants to do whatever she needs to do to get him back in the home.

WELLNESS EXERCISE

This chapter engaged you in learning skills for building rapport and trust with clients. The content and skills practice were meant to challenge you to develop listening skills founded on a basis of self-awareness, social justice, and a willingness to be vulnerable with yourself and others. In her TED talk, Julia Galef (posted in 2016) suggests several qualities that are important for successful practitioners: curiosity, openness, and being grounded. Practitioners who work from the stance of curiosity find pleasure in learning new information even if it contradicts something they originally thought was true (Galef, 2016). They also work from a perspective of openness such that they are willing to test their own beliefs (Galef, 2016). Finally, successful clinicians are grounded in that they do not bind their own self-worth to being right or wrong about a topic (Galef, 2016). I invite you to watch Julia's Ted Talk, *Why you think you're right—even if you're wrong*, by following the link that follows or searching for the title of it in your Web browser. What do you need to do to develop the *scout mindset and how will this help you become a stronger clinical interviewer*? Julia Galef's Ted Talk (posted June 2016): https://www.ted.com/talks/julia_galef_why_you_think_you_re_right_even_if_you_re_wrong?language=en

Clinical interviewing is strenuous work. Practitioners are privy to the private lives of individuals who are suffering on some level, and this makes wellness a necessary and required skill associated with clinical interviewing. Helping professionals, such as social workers, clinical psychologists, and other counselors, tend to carry large caseloads and work long hours with little or no time to promote their own wellness through stress reduction and wellness. In addition, helping professionals serve some of society's most vulnerable people who present with problems related to trauma, addictions, homelessness, and chronic mental illness, to name a few. As a result of these conditions, helping professionals are prone to high rates of work-related stress and burnout (Azar, 2000; Figley, 1995, 2002). This burnout and stress have a negative impact on their capacity to serve clients (Pearlman & Saakvitne, 1995) and on their longevity in the profession (Paris & Hoge, 2009).

As you embark on developing your clinical interviewing skills, I invite you to simultaneously build skills and habits for wellness. Therefore, each chapter of this book concludes with a wellness exercise or tip. The tip for this chapter is "honor joy in your life" and involves rewatching Media Clip 3: Oprah Winfrey interviewing Dr. Brene Brown, PhD, a social work educator and researcher who studies and writes about vulnerability. Unlike the first time you watched it, earlier in the chapter, you will want to be sure your device is not muted (https://www.youtube.com/watch?v=RKVoBWSPfOw). As you watch it, consider your own experience of joy: Do you also have the reflex of "fearing joy" that Dr. Brown discusses? What can you do to combine joy with gratitude in your life in order to avoid the "fear of joy"? Make a plan for noticing when you experience joy and finding gratitude in it.

RESOURCES FOR CREATING DELIVERABLES FOR ONLINE TEACHING AND LEARNING

Each of the skills exercises in this book lends itself to online deliverables for those who teach interviewing skills in the online environment. The following tips are meant to assist in transforming them from classroom-based activities to online teaching activities.

Tip 1: Set clear online expectations for each skills exercise so that students can complete them with limited input from the instructor. The simplest way to do this is to create concrete objectives about what students will be able to do as a result of completing each deliverable.

Tip 2: Make deliverables different than assignments such that deliverables are a means for students to demonstrate that they have completed the readings, whereas assignments demonstrate integrated learning that combines the readings and other course activities.

Tip 3: Assign points for the deliverables, but do not grade them. Recall that in a face-to-face classroom setting, students work in small groups to complete role plays, but these are not graded. In the online environment, deliverables become similar to those small-group role plays and do not need to be graded. However, assigning points is imperative so that the online students know that you expect them to complete the deliverables; you are online to monitor in the way the classroom instructor monitors small-group role plays.

Tip 4: Consider the amount of time it takes for students to complete the readings and deliverables such that this amounts to the amount of time they might spend in a face-to-face classroom. If 1 week of face-to-face class time is 2 hours, then strive to have your online readings and deliverable for each week equal to about 2 hours.

Tip 5: Break down the skills exercises into shortened segments that students complete and gain feedback back on prior to starting the next step of the exercise. For example, the skills exercise in this chapter on listening with person-centered values has two parts and smaller sections within each part such that it could become four deliverables in an online course. Completing the entire exercise for one online assignment or deliverable would overwhelm the students. Instead, break the first step into two parts so that first the students read the case example of Joan and write two paragraphs to respond to the prompt included in that step, "*As you read the case example, be aware of and makes notes for yourself on what the case circumstances call up in you: What feelings arise? What thoughts arise?*" After the students receive your comments and challenges to the thinking they demonstrated in that paragraph, they are ready for the next deliverable. The next deliverable is created from the second prompt in the first step of the exercise in which the students are required to complete a threaded discussion with the other students in the course in which they choose to take the side of either Joan (the parent) or one of her children and enter one comment into the discussion board about the reasons they take sides with that person. Then have each student respond to the comments of two other students who took the side of a different person in the case example and with those comments demonstrate how they allowed their classmates' comments to influence the way they think about the case example. For the second part of that skills exercise, assign students in your online class to small groups of three or four students and have them use the collaborative feature of your online learning platform to meet with you and hold a discussion on "How they will use person-centered values of genuineness, unconditional positive regard, and empathy to build rapport with Joan."

Tip 6: If the effort you need to put into assessing a deliverable that you create from the skills practice exercises in this book feels overwhelming to you as an instructor, then it will clearly be too overwhelming for students in an online learning environment. Use those skills exercises as assignments for students to demonstrate their integrated learning.

REFERENCES

Azar, S. T. (2000). Preventing burnout in professionals and paraprofessionals who work with child abuse and neglect cases: A cognitive behavioral approach to supervision. *In Session: Psychotherapy in Practice, 56*(5), 643–663.

Figley, C. R. (Ed.) (1995). *Compassion fatigue: Coping with secondary traumatic stress disorder in those who treat the traumatized.* New York: Brunner/Mazel.

Figley, C. R. (Ed.) (2002). *Treating Compassion Fatigue.* New York: Routledge.

Galaf, J. (2016). Ted Talk. https://www.ted.com/talks/julia_galef_why_you_think_you_re_right_even_if_you_re_wrong?language=en

Goleman, D. (1998). *Working with emotional intelligence*. New York, NY: Bantam Books.

Maskell, J. (2016). *The evolution of medicine: Join the movement to solve chronic disease and fall back in love with medicine*. Bedford, MA: Knew Publishing.

McKenzie, F. (2011). *Understanding and managing and the therapeutic relationship*. New York, NY: Oxford University Press.

McKenzie, F., & Nicotera, N. (in press). *Interviewing for the helping professions: A relational approach*. New York, NY: Oxford University Press.

Paris, M., & Hoge, M. A. (2009). Burnout in the mental health workforce: A review. *Journal of Behavioral Health Services & Research, 37*(4), 519–528.

Pearlman, L. A., & Saakvitne (1995). *Trauma and the Therapist: Counter Transference and Vicarious Traumatization in Psychotherapy with Incest Survivors*. W. W. Norton & Company, New York.

Rogers, C. (1957). The necessary and sufficient conditions of therapeutic personality change. *Journal of Consulting Psychology, 21*(2), 95–103.

Rogers, C. (2007). The necessary and sufficient conditions of therapeutic personality change. *Psychotherapy: Theory, Research, Practice, Training, 44*(3), 240–248.

Sue, D., Capodilupo, C., Torino, G., Bucceri, J., Holder, A., Nadal, K., & Esquilin, M. (2007). Racial microagressions in everyday life: Implications for clinical practice. *American Psychologist, 62*(4), 271–286.

Sue, D. (2010a). *Microaggressions in everyday life: Race, gender, and sexual orientation*. Hoboken, NJ: Wiley and Sons.

Sue, D. (2010b). *Microaggressions and marginality: Manifestation, dynamics, and impact*. Hoboken, NJ: Wiley and Sons.

2

Skills for Ethical Interviewing

THIS CHAPTER ADDRESSES skills that clinical interviewers use for implementing informed consent, confidentiality, and duty to warn or report on suicidal risk, homicidal intentions, and suspected child/elder abuse. It also covers the ethical issues of ensuring that practitioners describe their level of competence and practice modalities to clients as well as practice within professional boundaries and use the power of their position in ethical ways. These ethics and values arise from the various standards developed by the professional associations of helping professionals such as social workers, psychologists, mental health counselors, and nurses, to name a few.

Although the components of informed consent, confidentiality, and competence are common across different helping professions, each profession has nuanced ways in which it articulates its views on ethics and values related to power and social justice. The social work profession has specific standards on cultural competence (National Association of Social Workers, 2006). You are encouraged to read the values and ethics statements associated with your field of practice. For example, psychologists follow the American Psychological Association (APA) Code of Ethics (http://www.apa.org/ethics/code/index.aspx) and nurses apply the guidelines set out by the American Nursing Association (ANA) (http://www.nursingworld.org/codeofethics). This chapter addresses ethics from the perspective of social work Codes of Ethics and Values (e.g., National Association of Social Workers [NASW], http://www.socialworkers.org/pubs/Code/code.asp; Canadian Association of Social Workers [CASW], http://www.casw-acts.ca/en/

what-social-work/casw-code-ethics; International Association of Schools of Social Work [IASSW]; and International Federation of Social Workers [IFSW] http://cdn.ifsw.org/assets/ifsw_65044-3.pdf).

INFORMED CONSENT, COMPETENCE, AND CONFIDENTIALITY

Provisions for informed consent, competence, and confidentiality occur prior to initiating services and are typically described only second to greeting a client and establishing minimal rapport. The components of informed consent include a description and purpose of the services being offered, the potential risks involved, other options for treatment, the client's right to end or refuse services at any time, associated costs, and any limits of service related to an insurer. Practitioners cover the element of competence when they describe their credentials, training, and the methods they tend to use in therapy. Sometimes paperwork that covers informed consent and confidentiality also includes basic details about a practitioner's competence.

Confidentiality includes not revealing details about a client to any third party unless the client has provided written consent for a specific individual, health or medical provider, agency, or other organization such as a school. Even when a client provides consent for this purpose. the practitioner should only share details that are expressly relevant to the individual with whom they are sharing about that client. Confidentiality also requires that practitioners maintain written or electronic files about a client with the upmost security. Clients need to be aware of limits to confidentiality such that practitioners do not need written or verbal consent to reveal intent to commit suicide or homicide or reports of suspected child abuse or neglect and, in some states, suspected elder abuse or neglect.

Depending on the practice setting, clients may be given paperwork that covers informed consent and confidentiality to read and sign as part of an intake process or at the point of appointment check-in with a receptionist. In these cases, it is incumbent upon the practitioner who meets with the client to review this material and ensure that the client comprehends what she or he has signed because intake workers and/or receptionists are not always trained to provide this level of detail or provided the luxury of time to ensure client comprehension. In addition, the NASW Code of Ethics stipulates provisions for those who do not have the capacity to read a written version of informed consent and confidentiality such that the content is delivered verbally or translated, depending on client needs (National Association of Social Workers, 2008).

There are also provisions for ensuring that a legal third party is available for informed consent when clients do not have the cognitive or mental capacity to provide it. This includes ensuring that the third party has the best interests of the client at heart, in conjunction with providing a verbal explanation to the client in appropriate language. For example, in the state where I did clinical social work with children, youth, and families, the parents/legal guardians signed the formal consent for any child who was 13 years old or younger. However, I always provided verbal details in age-graded ways to the child or youth. If a client is in a clinical setting on an involuntary basis, the practitioner is still required to share details about the services and provide information for any possible service that the client can refuse when she or he has not volunteered for treatment (National Association of Social Workers, 2008).

Skills Practice—Competence

- Read the following case example of an exchange between an experienced practitioner and a new client at an initial session.
- Next type out or write down what you would say as the practitioner to communicate your competence to a new client.

Following are suggestions for creating what you would say:

1. If you are a student, it can help to start by identifying yourself as an intern who is earning a [M.S.W., M.A. in Counseling, etc.] at [name of institution].
2. You may want to let the client know how long you have been interning (e.g., This is the first year of my internship).
3. How you describe your competence and the way you work with clients will depend on how long you have been studying for your degree and the discipline you are studying.
4. If you are unsure about how to describe the way you work with clients, talk with your clinical supervisor or professors about how to articulate your practice.
   - After you type or write out what you would say, pair up with a classmate or colleague and take turns saying it to each other as if you were with a client. In other words, do not read verbatim what you wrote but instead learn to take it off the paper and into your head so you can say it with ease and comfort.
   - Use a computer, tablet, or cell phone and make an audiovisual recording of yourself as you practice this with a classmate or colleague. Play it back to watch and listen to how you sound. Make changes and adjustments based on your self-critique.

Case Example

The following initial session with a new client demonstrates how a clinician might communicate her or his competence. After the initial greetings and welcomes to the office and sitting down, the practitioner might begin in the following manner.

PRACTITIONER: Well, Jim, I remember from our phone conversation that you wanted to come in to talk about your marriage and some general concerns about your life. Did I understand that correctly?

JIM: Yeah, that's right.

PRACTITIONER: I want to hear more about that today, but before we get started, I want to let you know a little about me and how I practice and review the paperwork that you signed while you were in the waiting room and see if you have any questions about it.

JIM: Okay, that would be good. I have been to counseling before, so I am not new to it.

PRACTITIONER: Well, Jim, I want to first let you know that I am a licensed clinical social worker and earned my master in social work degree in 1995, so I have been in practice for quite some time. I like to stay on top of new techniques for how I can best help clients, so I also attend conferences and trainings every year (pause with silence to see if Jim has any response)

JIM: What do you mean by techniques?

PRACTITIONER: Well, in graduate school I was trained to help clients build on their strengths to make changes and also to help people make change by shifting the way they think and act toward themselves and the people around them. I still use that technique and I also like to work with clients to build on what keeps them going, even in the face of problems, as a way to build solutions and make lasting change. Recently, I have also been using techniques that help clients make a connection between their mind and body so they learn to manage how they feel and react so they can handle the ups and downs that life brings over the course of a lifetime. I really see my role as putting myself out of a job. That is, you and I will collaborate to decide what you want to be different because we worked together and help you develop the skills so you can make the changes you want and not need to work with me anymore.

JIM: You mean there will come a time when I won't need counseling?

PRACTITIONER: That is truly the goal here, Jim. It is kind of like how you take care of your physical health. Unless you have a chronic condition, like severe allergies that require regular visits to the doctor for allergy shots, you mostly maintain your health by eating right, exercising, and getting enough sleep. Taking care of your feelings and thoughts by working with a social worker or other counselor is similar. The goal is for you to build the strategies that work for you to cope with problems on your own as they arise and only return to therapy, if those coping strategies stop working.

JIM: Well, that makes sense to me and is a relief. I have a friend who has been in counseling for 10 years and does not seem to get any better.

Skills Practice—Informed Consent and Confidentiality

- Watch the following role-play example of an initial session in which the helping professional describes informed consent and confidentiality. This example is not perfect, so listen carefully for what the practitioner could do differently. https://www.youtube.com/watch?v=ANs9s7_u8SE
- After watching the media clip, respond to the following questions:
  1. The practitioner summarizes her role as a mandatory reporter. What would you add to it to be sure that the client clearly understands the specific details she is required to report?
  2. The practitioner provides some information about the agency's fee schedule. What else should she add from the list of items noted earlier in this chapter that ought to be shared during the informed consent process?
  3. In addition to confidentiality and informed consent, the practitioner provides an example of how she works with clients. What did she need to add to fully cover her competence?
  4. The practitioner also asks the client if she has been in counseling before and what she has tried to do to resolve her concerns before coming to the appointment. These are important elements in a first session, even though they are not required in the ethics and values statements for helping professionals. Why are these important elements?
- Now pair up with a classmate or colleague and take turns being the practitioner and client so each of you has an opportunity to deliver details about informed consent and confidentiality. Try it several times so that each of you feels comfortable with this content.
- Use a computer, tablet, or cell phone and make an audiovisual recording of yourself as you practice this with a classmate or colleague. Play it back to watch and listen to how you sound. Make changes and adjustments based on your self-critique.

ETHICAL BOUNDARIES, POWER, AND SOCIAL JUSTICE
Boundaries and Power

Helping professionals are trusted with many intimate details about a client's life, such as experiences of sexual abuse or suicide attempts at times of great despair, and we have contact with people when they may be at their most vulnerable. Maintaining healthy and professional boundaries is imperative for the strength of the helping relationship that best serves the client. The helping relationship is always meant to serve the client and not cater to the needs of the clinician. In addition, society imbues helping professionals with power and authority by virtue of an advanced academic degree and training and their capacity to diagnose clients. It is this power and access to a person's intimate life stories that make the clinician's self-awareness—in part described by the Rogerian concept of *genuineness* (Rogers, 2007) in Chapter 1—and wellness so important.

The standard boundary that practitioners may never have sex with a client is quite well known and so, too, is the boundary that our clients cannot become our friends or family, and our friends and family cannot become our clients. It is incumbent upon the helping professional to uphold these and other ethical boundaries. If a client you have been working with invites you to see a movie with her, it should be clear to you, as the clinician, that you must say no without leaving any ambiguity about the reason.

Practitioners who work and live in small towns or within small identity groups to which they belong, such as a transgender clinician who serves clients in the trans-community, are challenged with maintaining personal boundaries in a different way. In these cases, it is helpful for the practitioner to bring up the fact that the small town or small community of identity means that they may see each other outside of the counseling sessions and discuss how the client wants to handle it. A general stance is for the clinician to tell the client that they will ignore them unless the client speaks to the practitioner first. In that case, you and the client may also decide on a plan for clear boundaries, such that a wave or hello is okay, but not a conversation beyond the wave or hello. This kind of plan is something you will need to develop with the client, based on your best judgement call and in consultation with your clinical supervisor.

Boundaries related to clinicians revealing personal information about themselves to clients, more commonly called self-disclosure, is also complicated and less definitive. The use of self-disclosure is always a judgement call that the clinician makes. For example, the choice to display photos of your spouse or family in your office may depend on the population you serve or the rules of the agency where you work. In addition, responding to personal questions that a client may ask is also a judgement call on the part of the practitioner. There are no hard and fast rules for what to disclose, but the decision on whether or not to self-disclose should be based on the client's well-being and the practitioner's self-awareness as to the purpose of the self-disclosure.

Skill Practice—Self-Disclosure

- Read the following clinical interview in which a practitioner uses self-disclosure in a way that is not helpful for the client.
- Discuss the interview with a group of classmates or colleagues and a clinical supervisor or professor and identify how you could tell that this use of self-disclosure was not for the purpose of helping the client.

- Re-create the interview dialogue: first so that the interviewer does not answer the client's question and then so that the interviewer does answer the client's question, but in a way that is beneficial to the client.
- Re-create the interview dialogue as if the interviewer's parents had not divorced: first so that the interviewer does not answer the client's question and then so that the interviewer does answer the client's question.
- Which of the re-created dialogues are you most comfortable with and why?
- Make a list of the kinds of personal questions you most fear being asked by a client. This could be as basic as your age, faith, and if you have children, or it could be as complex as your personal history of trauma, addiction, or criminal action. Now consider how you would respond and discuss this with a trusted supervisor or professor.

The following is interview dialogue from the first session between a 16-year-old male client, Matt, and a 35-year-old male school social worker in which Matt shares his concerns about his parents' divorce (McKenzie, 2011, pp. 308–310; McKenzie & Nicotera, in press).

INTERVIEWER: Hi, Matt. I'm glad you could get out of study hall to see me today.

MATT: No problem, I really wanted to come to see you.

INTERVIEWER: So, I understand that your parents are going through a divorce.

MATT: Yeah, it really sucks.

INTERVIEWER: Well, you know my parents divorced when I was your age, and I really had a hard time with it, too. I know what you're going through.

MATT: Yeah, what was your parents' divorce like?

INTERVIEWER: My dad was an alcoholic, and my mom couldn't take it anymore so she started having an affair with one of our neighbors down the street. It was very awkward.

MATT: Boy, that must have been a pretty tough thing. How did you handle it?

INTERVIEWER: Well, I needed to get away from all of the craziness, so I started using drugs and drinking.

MATT: Did your parents find out about it?

INTERVIEWER: Eventually they did. They made me go to drug rehab. That was really intense and I hated it at the time, but when I think about it now, it might have been the best thing.

MATT: Well, my situation doesn't seem like it is anything as bad as yours. Maybe I should just suck it up and deal with it.

INTERVIEWER: Everybody's life is different, Matt. Let's talk about your situation.

MATT: My folks just told me last week that they were getting a divorce. I didn't see it coming; I thought they were getting along.

INTERVIEWER: Yeah, with my parents I wasn't a bit surprised. I just had a hard time being in the middle of it. You know, my mom wanted to talk about my dad, and my dad after he had been drinking would start crying with me about my mom. It was really tough.

MATT: Like I said, my situation doesn't seem anywhere near as bad as yours.

INTERVIEWER: Well, maybe not, Matt, but tell me how you're feeling about it.

MATT: I'm confused right now, and sort of angry I think, but I'm not sure why.

INTERVIEWER: I got real angry with my folks. I thought they were both acting kind of immature. Do you feel that way about your parents?

MATT: Like I said before, I'm not exactly sure how I feel, but I knew I needed to talk to someone about it. That's why I came to see you.

INTERVIEWER: Well, I'm glad you did, Matt. Talking these things out can be really helpful.

MATT: I hope so.

INTERVIEWER: Sure, it will. Let's meet again tomorrow to talk about it some more.

MATT: OK. But what should I do about how I'm feeling?

INTERVIEWER: Well, you know that I just used drugs to get away from the feelings. I wouldn't suggest that.

Social Justice

As noted earlier in this chapter, ethics related to social justice vary by the guidelines of the different helping professions. "Social workers promote social justice and social change with and on behalf of clients. 'Clients' is used inclusively to refer to individuals, families, groups, organizations, and communities. Social workers are sensitive to cultural and ethnic diversity and strive to end discrimination, oppression, poverty, and other forms of social injustice" (National Association of Social Workers, 2008, Preamble).

The ethic of social justice takes two paths: (1) the practitioner's lifelong journey toward cultural capacity that includes unlearning denigrating stereotypes toward people based on ethnicity/race, gender, faith, ability, sexual orientation, gender identity, age, and social class, and (2) the practitioner's lifelong journey of figuring out how and when to challenge colleagues and clients when they hear them making stereotyping and denigrating comments. In Chapter 1, I covered material on the role that microaggressions play in disrupting the therapeutic relationship, when a practitioner lacks the self-awareness to recognize when she or he has harmed a client with a comment or question that unintentionally stereotypes and insults a client because of the client's ethnicity/race, sexual orientation, gender identity, disability, religion, social class, or age, among others (Sue, 2007, 2010a, 2010b). This material relates to the first path of practitioner self-awareness and growth in cultural capacity. However, Chapter 1 of this book only scratches the surface in moving you toward gaining cultural capacity, and you are encouraged to read other sources as well as attend training and workshops focused on unlearning the stereotypes and denigrating attitudes that are so prevalent in society (Hill Collins, 2000; hooks, 1984; McIntosh, 1988, 1989; McKenzie & Nicotera, in press; Nicotera & Kang, 2009; Nicotera & Walls, 2010; Nicotera, Walls, & Lucero, 2010; Sue, Capodilupo, Torino, et al., 2007; Sue, 2010a, 2010b; Tatum, 1997). Some professional codes of ethics state that practitioners seek out this kind of education and growth such as the Code of Ethics for the National Association of Social Workers, which states: "Social workers should obtain education about and seek to understand the nature of social diversity and oppression with respect to race, ethnicity, national origin, color, sex, sexual orientation, age, marital status, political belief, religion, and mental or physical disability" (Code 1.05, http://www.socialworkers.org/pubs/code/code.asp).

In this chapter, I focus on the second path toward ethical clinical practice, which is the practitioner's lifelong journey of figuring out how and when to challenge colleagues and clients when they hear them making stereotyping and denigrating comments. Professional codes of ethics express this pathway such as the Social Work Code of Ethics that covers discrimination: "Social workers should not practice, condone, facilitate, or collaborate with any form of discrimination on the basis of race, ethnicity, national origin, color, sex, sexual orientation, age, marital status, political belief, religion, or mental or physical disability" (Code 4.02, http://www. socialworkers.org/pubs/code/code.asp).

Similarly, the American Psychological Association Code of Ethics states the following about discrimination: "In their work-related activities, psychologists do not engage in unfair discrimination based on age, gender, gender identity, race, ethnicity, culture, national origin, religion, sexual orientation, disability, socioeconomic status or any basis proscribed by law" (3.01, http://www.apa.org/ethics/code/index.aspx).

Challenging stereotyping statements that colleagues and clients make is a learned skill that is on par with all the clinical interviewing skills covered in this book. There are not many models for how to do this with assertiveness and grace; it only comes with practice and forethought. However, an absence of models does not release us from attempting to challenge harmful and hurtful comments that use stereotypes to oppress and denigrate people based on targeted identities. As the "Ethicist" wrote in his column in response to a reader's question, "What do I do when customers make racist comments?," not responding to such comments suggests that you are in agreement with the statement or at least that their comment "falls within the range of respectable opinion" (Appiah, 2016, p. 3).

In some cases, being curious is the first step to challenging outright discriminatory and/or subtle microaggressive comments you might hear based on racism, sexism, ableism, and so forth. Curiosity leads you to ask questions about the validity of a biased statement with the goal of having an educational conversation. For example, you might ask, "How did you decide that all [name of any stereotyped, targeted group] are [any general stereotype about that group such as being on drugs, being a single parent]." In essence, with this strategy you are working toward refuting someone's biased belief as having no basis in fact. This will work with some people and not with others, but it is worth a try.

Sometimes, however, you realize that curiosity is not the right step and you need to choose a more direct route, such as stating that you are offended by what the person is saying. For example, "I know some people believe that, but honestly, I find it offensive." Another way to put it is, "It hurts my heart to hear this kind of stereotype that I know hurts people I care about." The "Ethicist's" (Appiah, 2016) column on what to do when customers make racist comments provides another response, which he provides for the context of a racist comment and you can extrapolate to include other identity groups: "If you knew more about the lives of black Americans you wouldn't say that" (p. 3). If you are at a loss for how to directly challenge someone who makes offensive, biased comments about targeted groups, you can always rely on your professional code of ethics in support of calling the person out on his or her comment: "I know it will likely make you feel uncomfortable, but my professional code of ethics requires me to let you know that what you just said isn't actually true, and in fact hurts people."

As you read these examples, you may be thinking, *I can imagine challenging a colleague who makes an ageist, racist, or sexist comments, but my clients did not come to therapy for their biased views. Do I really need to challenge them, too?* In reality, if you allow clients' discriminatory and microaggressive comments to go unchallenged, you not only suggest that you agree with them but also do them a disfavor of learning from a teachable moment. In part, the client's presenting problem may be compounded by his or her biased beliefs and attitudes. In part, your willingness to challenge that client provides him or her with an opportunity to change and become a stronger, more socially adept human being, and is that not one of the many reasons that people seek out therapy in the first place?

Skills Practice—Social Justice

Suggesting an exercise for practicing the skill of challenging stereotyped comments toward people whose identities are targeted by racism, transphobia, sexism, ageism, and ableism, to name a few, is tough because I do not want to write harmful comments as examples. However, these kinds of comments are alive and well, and you will hear them in the lines of characters in movies and television shows as well as from news reported and commentators. In addition, because none of us is immune to the societal lessons that teach us to be biased, there are likely biased comments rolling around in your thoughts, even as you read this chapter. Therefore, the skills practice is to become aware of the comments that you hear in the media and in your own mind, and practice how to challenge them. It is best to practice this skills with someone who shares your own identities so that you are not traumatizing someone who is the target of such comments.

WELLNESS EXERCISE

Learning clinical interviewing skills and practicing them in real time with a class-mate or colleague as well as audio-recording them is a strenuous endeavor. Applying the ethics of social justice and challenging yourself to acknowledge when you mess up and voice a microaggresive comment is even more strenuous. You will make many mistakes on your journey. Learning compassion for yourself and others can be a great tool for this strenuous journey. Therefore, the wellness exercise offered here is a mindfulness compassion meditation. Compassion meditation involves a "reflective practice that teaches active examination of loving-kindness, empathy, and compassion towards loved ones, strangers, and enemies [and] employs a variety of mental restructuring and emotion producing practices with the goal of developing a calmness of mind that fosters acceptance and understanding of others" (Muraco & Raison, 2012, p. 3).

The compassion meditation offered here is simple and is fashioned from the com-passion meditation found on the University of New Hampshire health and coun-seling website, where you will scroll the offering to find the "Metta Meditation" https://www.unh.edu/healthservices/ohep/meditation or at https://www.youtube.com/watch?v=nRodohZ3iIw. To practice any kind of mindful meditation, first find a comfortable place where no one will disturb you for the next 5 to 10 minutes. Sit in a chair or on the floor or lay down so that you can be comfortable but not fall asleep. If you are sitting, be sure that your back is upright and not slouched so that the air can freely move in and out of your lungs as you inhale and exhale. Allow your head to gently lift to the sky, your shoulders to gently drop toward your elbows, and your feet to be gently planted on the floor. If it feels right, you then gently close your eyes; if you prefer to keep your eyes open, find a place to lower your gaze to so that your mind is not distracted by what you see around you.

Now breath in slowly and out slowly five to ten times so that your stomach rises away from your backbone when you inhale and sinks toward your backbone when you exhale. Take your time; there is no one to rush you, and there is not one right way to breath. Then, when you are ready, picture yourself as you are at this moment and, as you do, repeat the following statements to yourself:

> May you know peace.
> May your heart remain open.
> May you know the beauty of your own true nature.
> May you be healed.
> May you be a source of healing for others.

Now slowly inhale and exhale for a few breaths; and as you do, picture someone you care about—it might be a friend, a spouse, or even a companion animal such as your cat. Hold this image in your mind as you once again repeat the phrases, sending compassion toward the person or companion animal in your life.

Now slowly inhale and exhale for a few breaths and, as you do, picture someone you do not know very well but come into contact with on a regular basis. Hold this image in your mind as you once again repeat the phrases, sending compassion toward the person.

Now slowly inhale and exhale for a few breaths and, as you do, picture someone with whom you have a conflict or difficulty. Hold this image in your mind as you once again repeat the phrases, sending compassion toward that person.

Now slowly inhale and exhale for a few breaths and, as you do, picture the world as the people in it or as if you were imagining a view of the Earth from space. Hold this image in your mind as you once again repeat the phrases, sending compassion toward the world.

Now breath in slowly and out slowly five to ten times, so that your stomach rises away from your backbone when you inhale and sinks toward your backbone when you exhale. When you are ready, open your eyes.

REFERENCES

Appiah, K. (2016). What should you do when customers make racists remarks? *New York Times,* December 14, 2016.

Hill Collins, P. (2000). *Black feminist thought: Knowledge, consciousness, and the politics of empowerment.* New York, NY: Routledge.

Hooks, b. (1984). *Feminist theory: From margin to center.* Boston, MA: South End Press.

Macintosh, P. (1988). White privilege and male privilege: A personal accounting of coming to see correspondence through work in women's studies. In M. L. Anderson & P. H. Collins (Eds.) *Race, class and gender* (pp. 76–87). Belmont, CA: Wadsworth.

McIntosh, P. (1989). White privilege: Unpacking the invisible knapsack. *Peace and Freedom*, July/August, 10–12.

McKenzie, F. (2011). *Understanding and managing the therapeutic relationship*. New York, NY: Oxford University Press.

McKenzie, F., & Nicotera, N. (in press). *Interviewing for the helping professions: A relational approach*. New York, NY: Oxford University Press.

Muraco, J. A., & Raison, C. L. (2012). Compassion training as a pathway to lifelong health and wellbeing. *Frances McClelland Institute for Children, Youth, and Families Research, 4*(3). Tucson, AZ: The University of Arizona. Retrieved from https://mcclellandinstitute.arizona.edu/sites/mcclellandinstitute.arizona.edu/files/ResearchLink%20Vol.%204.%20No.%203.pdf.

National Association of Social Workers. (2006). Standards and indicators of cultural competence in social work practice. Retrieved from http://www.socialworkers.org/practice/standards/NASWCulturalStandardsIndicators2006.pdf

National Association of Social Workers. (2008). *Code of ethics of the National Association of Social Workers*. Washington, DC. NASW Press.

Nicotera, N., & Kang, H. (2009). Beyond diversity courses: Strategies for integrating critical consciousness across social work curriculum. *Journal of Teaching in Social Work, 29*(2), 188–203.

Nicotera, N., & Walls, N. E. (2010). Challenging perceptions of academic research as bias free: Promoting a social justice framework in social work research methods courses. *Journal of Teaching in Social Work, 30*(3), 334–350.

Nicotera, N., Walls, N. E., & Lucero, N. (2010). Understanding practice issues with American Indians: Listening to practitioner voices. *Journal of Ethnic and Cultural Diversity in Social Work, 19*(3), 195–216.

Rogers, C. (2007). The necessary and sufficient conditions of therapeutic personality change. *Psychotherapy: Theory, Research, Practice, Training, 44*(3), 240–248.

Sue, D. W., Capodilupo, C., Torino, G., Bucceri, J., Holder, A., Nadal, K., & Esquilin, M. (2007). Racial microaggressions in everyday life: Implications for clinical practice. *American Psychologist, 62*(4), 271–286

Sue, D. W. (2010a). *Microaggressions in everyday life: Race, gender, and sexual orientation*. Hoboken, NJ: Wiley.

Sue, D. W. (2010b). *Microaggressions and marginality: Manifestation, dynamics, and impact*. Hoboken, NJ: Wiley.

Tatum, B. (1997). *Why are all the Black kids sitting together in the cafeteria? And other conversations about race*. New York, NY: Basic Books.

3

Skills for Obtaining the Initial Story

REGARDLESS OF WHETHER the stories are positive, negative, or neutral, we create our lives and reactions to our lives through the stories we tell ourselves, the stories we tell others, and the stories others tell us about ourselves. When clients reach out to a clinical social worker or a mental health counselor for assistance, their stories have typically become focused in the negative, the impossible, or some other tale suggesting an unsolvable problem. By the time clients reach you, they have likely tried many ways to resolve the story that infringes on their life, and many times they have lost sight of the positive stories or stories of possibility. Your role as a mental health practitioner is to learn the clients' stories, to assist them in uncovering the layers of the stories that influence their lives, and to help them remember or reinvent stories of possibility.

This chapter addresses four foundational clinical interviewing skills that are essential for obtaining a client's initial story, ensuring that the client hears his or her own story and that you comprehend it in the way the client would intend. The skills addressed here are also used throughout your work with clients, but they come into sharp relief here for gaining the initial story. The skills for building rapport that you learned in Chapter 1 set the stage for the client wanting to tell you his or her story and you will use them in conjunction with the skills covered here. Subsequent chapters will address other skills that lead you deeper into clients' stories. The following sections present open and closed questions, paraphrasing, and summarizing, combined with exercises that challenge you to decide when you would use which skill to obtain the client's initial story.

OPEN AND CLOSED QUESTIONS: THE ROLE OF POWER

We use open and closed questions in our daily lives, whether we are asking about a product we intend to buy or having a conversation with a loved one. The daily use of these skills makes their use in clinical interviewing seem deceptively simple. However, when they are used for clinical interviewing, the practitioner needs to be keenly aware of the choices he or she makes for which type of question to use, when to use it, and the potential outcome of posing a question as closed or open. Clinicians must have a moment-by-moment awareness of how their position of power plays out in the process of asking questions. Power was discussed in detail in Chapters 1 and 2, but to reiterate here, being in a position of questioning to learn intimate details about a person's life without sharing that same vulnerability yourself is clearly a position of power. This professional boundary is necessary for a healthy and helpful relationship between mental health professional and client, and it simultaneously underscores the power differential that becomes amplified with the use of clinical questioning. Depending on the scenario, it can be helpful to make this typically undiscussed power and questioning more obvious by being direct with the client about it. For example, you may want to tell a client, "I realize that I will be asking you a lot of questions as I get to know you and understand your concerns and strengths. Everyone has different reactions to being asked questions. If I ask you any questions that seem odd or off base to you, please feel free to tell me."

Use of power during clinical questioning also entails posing questions with the intent to learn important information that is deemed necessary for helping, and not because the clinician is simply curious. The idea of curiosity is a tough one for the mental health professional. On the one hand, curiosity is an important asset for obtaining the details of a client's story. On the other hand, prurient or voyeuristic curiosity is unwarranted and can only serve to amplify the power of the clinician and make clients feel unsafe and uncomfortable. To make matters even more complex, the use of questioning and reaction to questioning is culturally bound. However, there is no recipe book for how to work with or interact with specific cultures, and culture is broadly defined to not only represent social identities (e.g., sexual orientation, age) and ethnicities but also includes familial and regional cultures. This is where reading a client's nonverbal responses to questions such as facial expressions and body language, as well as being aware of tone of voice, becomes even more important. If you observe that the client's tone of voice changes or his or her facial expression changes when you pose a particular question, then ask about it. For example, you might say, "I noticed that you seemed to frown when I asked about what is like to live where you live. Perhaps my question has made you uncomfortable. I apologize if that is the case." The clinician who is willing to make herself vulnerable by following up on a client's nonverbal reactions and offering apologies or some other option for an openness to talking about how the questioning influences the client's experience is likely to deepen her rapport with the client. The key is that what seems like a common or simple question to one person, such as yourself, may seem like a complicated or invasive question to someone else. As the professional, it is your role to be observant, so you check in with clients if they seem reticent to respond and apologize as needed. At the same time, it is your role to pose questions or address issues that create discomfort in clients, as making change is most often uncomfortable. There is no rule book for which questions to ask or not to ask or when to ask them; you must rely on your keen sense of self-awareness, integrity, and client observation skills. As I tell my students, there is a common statement for when one wants to suggest that something is not that difficult. That statement is, "Well, it's not rocket science." However, clinical mental health practice *is* rocket science and perhaps even more difficult, as there are no specific equations for ensuring that what one does will lead to the expected result. With that caveat, we move into the practicalities of open and closed questioning skills.

Closed questions represent a frame for obtaining information in a truncated manner, such as seeking a simple yes or no response or a more specific response such as how old someone is, where that person lives, or if that person has children. Open questions are meant to elicit a longer response that holds more story details. For example, you might follow a closed question asking someone where he or she lives with an open question such as "What is like to live there?"

Skills Practice—Open and Closed Questions: Part 1

- Watch the two Ted Talk Interviews by following the links provided or by typing the following titles into your Web browser; choose the link associated exactly with each of the titles "William Kamkwamba: How I built a windmill Ted Talk" (https://www.ted.com/talks/william_kamkwamba_on_building_a_windmill#t-228135) and next "Jane Fonda and Lily Tomlin: A hilarious celebration of lifelong female friendship Ted Talk" (https://www.ted.com/talks/jane_fonda_and_lily_tomlin_a_hilarious_celebration_of_lifelong_female_friendship#t-931381).
- Watch each Ted Talk and identify when the interviewer uses open questions and closed questions. Note how the interviewees respond to open and closed

questions. Do they respond with more detail for the open questions and less detail for the closed questions? Which style gives the interviewee more talk time—the use of open questions or the use of closed questions?

- Type or write out three open questions and three closed questions you would use in each interview and identify where in the interviews you would pose those questions. Also explain why you would use the questions at those junctures in the interviews.

Skills Practice—Open and Closed Questions: Part 2

- Work with another classmate or colleague and take turns creating an audiovisual recording of you interviewing each other about an agreed-upon topic for about 15 minutes each. Do not make up a therapy problem or setting. Be your real selves; the interview can be about anything you choose as long as it is *not* about a current personal problem or trauma for which you should seek professional counseling. If you do not have access to an audiovisual recording, then work in teams of three classmates or colleagues and take turns being the observer so that each observer makes notes during the interview itself about the topics listed in the next step.
- After the interviews are complete, ask the observer to share his or her notes on the following topics if you did not audiovisual record it; if you did create recordings, then watch them together or separately, and note how often each of you used open questions and closed questions when you were the interviewer. Also, note how the interviewee responded to open questions compared to closed questions: Does the interviewee give as much detail about his or her story regardless of the type of question you used? If so, what might it be about this interviewing situation that caused him or her to give details regardless of whether you used open or closed questions? How might this be different in a clinical setting with a client?

PARAPHRASING AND SUMMARIZING

The skill of paraphrasing is meant to let the client know you heard what he or she said to you and allow for the client to then correct it, if you did not quite grasp what he or she was saying. A paraphrase can also be used to bring an interview back to the topic, if the client seems to have gone off on a tangent. A paraphrase should replay the client's experiences or ideas without directly parroting them. That is, a paraphrase should not be so similar to what the client just said that he or she wonders if indeed you were actually listening. Instead, it should capture the essence of what the client said. The following excerpt from an interview between a client, Andrew, a successful helping professional at a psychiatric clinic, and a mental health practitioner (McKenzie, 2011, pp. 214–125; McKenzie & Nicotera, in press) provides examples of each of these instances. Note the label of paraphrase in brackets after each paraphrase that the interviewer uses.

> INTERVIEWER: Hello, Andrew. It's nice to meet you. I understand that you have been experiencing some difficulties at work.
>
> ANDREW: Yeah, I've been at this psychiatric facility for several years now. I'm doing quite well and have been promoted to a supervisory position.
>
> INTERVIEWER: Sounds like you've been successful. [**paraphrase**]
>
> ANDREW: That's not really the problem. You see, the longer I'm there, the more awkward I feel.
>
> INTERVIEWER: Can you explain to me what you mean, feeling awkward?
>
> ANDREW: Well, yes and no. I mean, I like everyone that I work with, and I seem to get along well with all of my coworkers and staff, but I just feel off. I can't put my finger on it.
>
> INTERVIEWER: That's OK; let's talk some more about those vague feelings. [**paraphrase**]
>
> ANDREW: Good, it's just that I'm usually very good about understanding myself and my instincts. I've been in therapy before, when I was a teenager, so I know the process. I also work in the field, so I really appreciate and respect the process. I know I'm stuck.
>
> INTERVIEWER: That's a good way to put it, I think, Andrew.
>
> ANDREW: Thanks.
>
> INTERVIEWER: So, you find yourself liking the people at work but also feeling awkward around them? [**paraphrase to get the interviewee back on the topic**]

A summarization covers more territory than a paraphrase and is typically used to pull together a series of ideas or different parts of a client's story. Sometimes this is done at the beginning of session to review what was covered in the previous session or a phone call prior to the session. At other times, it can be used to review a series of things a client shared if he or she has been talking for some time. In this instance, the goal may be to help a client focus on one issue at a time if he or she has been sharing a laundry list of concerns. Summarizations can also be used at the close of session to sum up what was covered during the entire session. At times, the use of a summarization at the end of session can also function as a launch for what the client wants to focus on in between the current session and the next session.

The following interview excerpt demonstrates an example of a summarization used at the beginning of a session to review what was discussed in the previous session and find out what the client wants to address in the current session (McKenzie, 2011, p. 141; McKenzie & Nicotera, in press). The client, Linda, has been working with the practitioner for several sessions and talking about concerns within her marriage and with her children as well as some issues related to her childhood.

INTERVIEWER: Hi, Linda. How have things been going since our last session?

LINDA: Oh, about the same. Nothing has changed, but at least there haven't been any major blowups since I saw you.

INTERVIEWER: I guess that's good [pauses]. We talked about a lot of things last week, including your present situation with your family, and a little bit about your childhood. Is there any particular thing you'd like to talk about today? [**summarization**]

This next interview excerpt between Al, a man who is dying, and a practitioner (McKenzie, 2011, pp. 218–221; McKenzie & Nicotera, in press) demonstrates the use of summarization of details from a previous session as well as for closing the session and launching an idea for something the client may choose to try or work on before the next session. The excerpt begins near the end of the session with Al discussing his regrets that he was not a better father.

AL: I think there have been times that I've been a good dad.

INTERVIEWER: Do you remember any times in particular?

AL: When the kids were younger, especially my first two sons, I remember taking them to an occasional baseball game. We all seemed to have fun. Sometimes we went fishing when we were on vacation. Those were good times, I think.

INTERVIEWER: Sounds like they were fun for you.

AL: Yeah, I think they were.

INTERVIEWER: So, what makes you think you weren't a good dad, Al?

AL: Well, you know, I mentioned that I was, or maybe I should say am, an alcoholic. I've been in recovery for a long time.

INTERVIEWER: I know you've mentioned that, and we've talked about it a bit. You started drinking in the navy, right? Then your drinking continued to escalate until you were in your fifties. How did this affect your relationship with your family? [**summarization from a previous session**]

AL: I know it did. You know I worked sales, and it was very stressful. I didn't have a college degree, but still did very well. But I'd come home every night, and I do mean every night, with a twelve pack of beer. I wouldn't pay much attention to the kids, just watch sports on TV and drink all twelve of those beers and more every night. If I ran out of beer, I'd start drinking the hard stuff; you know, whiskey. I would usually pass out on the couch and eventually make it to bed. My kids tell me that I was pretty abusive and scary. I wouldn't let them watch any of their shows, and I tended to criticize and belittle them a lot . . . at least that's what they tell me.

INTERVIEWER: So, you don't really remember much of this, except what your kids have told you?

AL: Oh, a little bit here and there. My wife remembers a lot of it and has told me that the kids are right. I've never really been much of a father to them, you see. I don't know if I really knew how, and to tell you the truth . . . I feel bad about this . . . I'm not sure I really wanted to have kids. My wife loves them to death, and they are her whole life. I have to admit that I have been jealous of them and her relationship with them.

INTERVIEWER: That's a very honest statement, Al. What is it like for you to tell me this?

AL: I feel embarrassed to tell you this, but I really want to get this out and try to make things better with my whole family.

INTERVIEWER: I appreciate your trusting me enough to tell me these things, Al. Our session is just about over for today, so we can pick this up when we meet the next time, if you choose. You mentioned some earlier memories when you felt you were being a good dad. However, you seem to suggest that this is outweighed by several regrets, mainly focused on how your drinking interfered with your relationship with your children, not really wanting to have children and ended up feeling jealous of the children's relationship with your wife. It sounds like you're committed to making things better with your whole family [**summarization for closing the session**]. In between now and our next session, what do you think about taking stock to decide if you want to begin this process and, if you do, how you might want to start, whether it is with one or more of your children and which ones, whether you want to include your wife in the process [**launching the client to think about where he wants to take this conversation and work**]? Whatever you decide, I am going to be here to support your choice and assist you in working through whatever you choose.

Skills Practice—Paraphrasing and Summarizing: Part 1

- Work in small groups of three or four to watch the following 4-minute Ted Talk by accessing the following link or the words "Ted Talk Try Something

New for 30 days" in your Web browser (http://www.ted.com/talks/matt_cutts_try_something_new_for_30_days).

- The talk is a monologue, so as you watch it, imagine that you are interviewing the speaker. As you watch it, create and write down three paraphrases for any parts of the monologue. Remember that a paraphrase does not parrot what the speaker says; instead, it brings together the essence of what the speaker is saying. Each person in the group should work independently to write his or her own paraphrases and not share them with each other until the next step.
- After everyone in the group has seen the Ted Talk and each has created three paraphrases, pass your list to the person on your right. When you have the paraphrases of one of the people in your group, read them to yourself and try to recall which part of the talk the paraphrase reflects. If you are not able to tell, then pass that one on to someone else in the group until someone can figure it out or the person who wrote it explains which part of the interview it covers.
- Now, as a whole group, write two summarizations: one for the first minute and thirty seconds or up to where the speaker tells about climbing Mt. Kilimanjaro and the other summarization for the rest of the talk. Remember, you are summarizing what the speaker says, not trying to completely reiterate everything said.

Skills Practice—Paraphrasing and Summarizing: Part 2

- Work with another classmate or colleague and take turns creating an audio-visual recording of you interviewing each other about an agreed-upon topic for about 15 minutes each. Do not make up a therapy problem or setting. Be your real selves; the interview ought to be about an experience you have had that your classmate or colleague does not know about. It can be anything you experience as long as it is *not* about a current personal problem or trauma for which you should seek professional counseling. When you are the interviewer, use paraphrasing to clarify aspects of your classmate's experience that are unclear to you and also to reflect what they are saying back to them, but in a more succinct way. If you do not have access to audiovisual recording, then work in teams of three classmates or colleagues and take turns being the observer to complete the next step.
- After the interviews are complete, watch them together or separately and note how often each of you used paraphrases when you were the interviewer. Also, note how the interviewee responded to the paraphrases: Did they give you more information when you were trying to use a paraphrase to clarify content? Did they correct you, if your paraphrase was incorrect?

Embarking on the journey of becoming a helping professional not only requires clinical interviewing skills but also requires developing healthy habits for wellness. In fact, there is a positive relationship between wellness and stress and wellness and quality of life. For example, wellness activities such as spending time with friends and/or family, taking walks, cooking and eating a healthy meal, meditating or praying, among others are related to lower stress and greater quality of life in first-year master of social work students (Nicotera, Crosby, Black, & Ross, in progress).

Your longevity as a helping professional depends on developing and maintaining habits of wellness. Helping professionals, such as social workers, clinical psychologists, and other counselors serve some of society's most vulnerable people who present with problems related to trauma, addictions, homelessness, and chronic mental illness, to name a few. Helping professionals also tend to carry large caseloads and work long hours with little or no time to promote their own wellness through stress reduction and wellness. As a result of these conditions, helping professionals are prone to high rates of work-related stress and burnout (Azar, 2000; Figley, 1995, 2002). This burnout and stress have a negative impact on their capacity to serve clients (Pearlman & Saakvitne, 1995) and on their longevity in the profession (Paris & Hoge, 2009). This makes developing habits for wellness equally important to developing excellent clinical interviewing skills. Therefore, this and each of the subsequent chapters has a section on wellness.

Some of you may already have habits of wellness, and your challenge will be to maintain them as you complete your graduate degree, professional training, or continue in your current position as a helping professional. Others may realize that they need to develop a wellness plan. If you are like many people, you may have a good sense of what you need to do for wellness, but often find it going by the wayside when your time is limited. However, taking 10 minutes each day for a walk, to meditate or pray, or to laugh with someone you care about can make a big difference in your stress and quality of life.

In an effort to develop or reinvigorate a current wellness program, I encourage you to rewatch the Ted Talk noted in the previous skills practice section "Try Something New for 30 days." As you watch it again, consider one small change you can make to develop or maintain wellness and make a commitment to do it for 30 days in a row. However, make it a small sustainable change; as the speaker in the Ted Talk notes, if you pick a small, feasible change, you will be more likely to maintain it. In fact, good clinical work helps clients to focus on making small changes and feeling successful about those before trying to make huge changes. It will also help if you find a buddy who wants to try make a small change for 30 days so you can support and motivate each other in the process. There is no time like the present to begin!

PRACTICING SOCIAL JUSTICE

The everyday awareness of social justice is also equally important to learning clinical interviewing skills. One way that you can begin to develop stronger social justice awareness is by thinking critically about the media you see and the events that happen around you each day. For example, think critically about the Ted Talk that you just rewatched, "Try Something New for 30 days." What activities does the speaker describe that require a certain level of social-economic class, physical ability, and access to leisure time? Although the idea of trying something new for 30 days is relevant to anyone, the content of the talk itself may not resonate with some people. This kind of critical thinking does not diminish the ideas of the Ted Talk as useful. Instead, it helps you to move beyond your own perspective, which is a key ingredient for opening your heart and mind to anyone whose social or cultural identity is targeted.

REFERENCES

Azar, S. T. (2000). Preventing burnout in professionals and paraprofessionals who work with child abuse and neglect cases: A cognitive behavioral approach to supervision. *In Session: Psychotherapy in Practice, 56*(5), 643–663.

Figley, C. R. (Ed.) (1995). *Compassion fatigue: Coping with secondary traumatic stress disorder in those who treat the traumatized.* New York, NY: Brunner/Mazel.

Figley, C. R. (Ed.) (2002). *Treating compassion fatigue.* New York, NY: Routledge.

McKenzie, F. (2011). *Understanding and managing and the therapeutic relationship.* New York, NY: Oxford University Press.

McKenzie, F., & Nicotera, N. (in press). *Interviewing for the helping professions: A relational approach.* New York, NY: Oxford University Press.

Nicotera, N., Crosby, Black, & Ross (in progress). *Self-care and wellness for the helping professions.*

Paris, M., & Hoge, M. A. (2009). Burnout in the mental health workforce: A review. *Journal of Behavioral Health Services & Research, 37*(4), 519–528.

Pearlman, L. A., & Saakvitne (1995). *Trauma and the therapist: Counter transference and vicarious traumatization in psychotherapy with incest survivors.* New York, NY: Norton.

4

Skills to Deepen the Telling and Understanding of the Story

THIS CHAPTER COVERS skills that are necessary for ensuring that you gain a deeper understanding of the client's story. When these skills are used with compassion and competence, they also challenge clients to consider the stories they tell in new and different hues. In other words, these skills take you and the client into a deeper telling and exploration of the story. As such, it is best to use these skills after you have built a strong rapport with the client and earned the client's trust in your competence and compassion. However, in the world of brief therapies and in some types of counseling, such as substance abuse treatment, these skills may be used earlier in the relationship.

PERSON-CENTERED APPROACH

The configuration of skills addressed in this chapter include uncovering and attending to emotion, eliciting meaning, and challenging incongruity. The tenets of Carl Rogers's person-centered approach (Rogers, 1995) are essential for implementing these skills. Rogers's person-centered approach to clinical practice and the core elements of his approach—*congruence, unconditional positive regard,* and *empathy*—remain active concepts for contemporary clinical practice (e.g., Rogers, 2007). The practice of these core elements requires what I call astute or wise self-awareness, especially as a means to practice from a social justice perspective. I succinctly discuss each of the elements here and address the role of obstacles to practicing them from a social justice stance.

Congruence

Rogers (1995) used words like *genuineness* and *authenticity* as synonyms for the term *congruence*. He suggested that clinicians be self-aware and present their authentic, genuine selves in the face of how a client's story unfolds (Rogers, 1995). This is not to suggest that the clinician should overstep professional boundaries and make a story or session all about oneself. Instead, it means being authentic in response to the client's story from a space of astute or wise self-awareness that reflects the emotion and content of the client's experience.

Unconditional Positive Regard

Rogers (1995) used words like *acceptance, caring,* and *support* in reference to his ideas about unconditional positive regard. He suggested that practitioners accept, without judgement, clients' expression of feelings and the stories of where they are in the moment. This is not to suggest that the clinician should approve of the actions of clients who seek or have been mandated to services as a result of causing harm, such as a death caused while driving under the influence of substances or for child abuse or a hate crime. Using acceptance, caring, and support so that clients can tell the stories that led to such actions does not imply approval of the actions. Instead, unconditional positive regard suggests communicating genuine caring for clients' healing and change process.

Empathy

Rogers (1995) described listening with empathy as the capacity to "walk a mile in someone else's shoes" so as to keenly sense the client's experiences and sentiments about his or her experiences and actions. It does not mean taking on and expressing the client's story as one's own story; instead, it means empathizing with circumstances and contexts that brought the client to be on a certain path. One does not need to become addicted to substances to walk a mile in the shoes of the client who is addicted to them. Instead, the clinician uses empathy to understand the intrapersonal, interpersonal, environmental, and social justice factors that played a role in the client's addiction.

CORE ELEMENTS OF THE PERSON-CENTERED APPROACH IN A
CONTEXT OF SOCIAL JUSTICE

Our understanding of social justice and the prevalence of microaggressions adds a new twist on the three elements of the person-centered approach: *congruence, unconditional positive regard,* and *empathy.* The component of astute self-awareness is key for considering the twist of social justice and microaggressions on Rogers's concepts. I define astute or wise self-awareness as (1) continual examination of how your views, beliefs, values, words, and actions are influenced by racism, sexism, transphobia, ageism, heterosexism, ableism, and fear of certain religions (e.g., Islamaphobia); (2) owning the fact that no one escapes the influence of these oppressive "isms"; and (3) active engagement in unlearning the messages, biases, and behaviors they promote in you. I draw my ideas about wise self-awareness from the concept of *cultural humility* (Tervalon & Murray-Garcia, 1998). This concept arises out of medical training to arm physicians with the capacity to overturn their "unintentional and intentional processes of racism, classism, homophobia, and sexism" (Tervalon & Murray-Garcia, 1998, pp. 117–118). Practicing from cultural humility "incorporates a lifelong commitment to self-evaluation and self-critique, to redressing the power imbalances in the patient–physician dynamic, and to developing mutually beneficial and nonpaternalistic clinical and advocacy partnerships with communities on behalf of individuals and defined populations" (Tervalon & Murray-Garcia, 1998, p. 117).

Cultural humility indicates a never-ending process of learning and unlearning stereotypes and listening for how each person expresses his or her culture(s) and identities. It is the idea that there is no recipe book from which to practice. For example, there is no one-size-fits-all way to practice with transgender clients any more than there is a one-size-fits-all way to practice with cisgender clients. Practitioners who provide services from an ethos of cultural humility are "flexible and humble enough to assess anew the cultural dimensions of the experiences of each patient . . . and to say that they do not know when they truly do not know" (Tervalon & Murray-Garcia, 1998, p. 119). Cultural humility is a foundation for practicing with wise self-awareness, and both are integral to applying Rogers's core elements from a social justice perspective.

UNCOVERING AND ATTENDING TO EMOTION

The skills for uncovering and attending to a client's emotions or feelings are typically referred to as *reflecting feelings* (Cummins, Sevel, & Pedrick, 2006; Evans, Hearn, Uhlemann, & Ivey, 2015; Ivey, 2007). Reflecting feelings involves listening for the client's use of feeling words and tone of voice as well as observing the client's facial and body language. At the most basic level, reflecting feelings involves paraphrasing the feeling content of a client's story. For example, a client may begin to describe the story of when her dog passed away and tears may come with the words. Reflecting feelings at a most basic level here would be acknowledging the tears and the likelihood that they indicate sadness by stating for example, "I see the tears and hear sadness as you talk about [name of dog]'s passing." However, there is risk in naming the tears and tone of voice as sadness, because the tears could also suggest something other than sadness, such as despair, loneliness, or regret.

To make matters more complex, another client may tell you about the death of his dog without any indication of related feelings, at least that you can hear or observe. This is because feeling expression is unique to each person telling the story and the experience related to it. How we express and hear feelings is linked to the ways in which we learned about feelings in our families and how we stayed true to or made changes to that early learning. Feeling expression is also related to socialization; for example, boys are often ridiculed for crying and girls who express anger are often silenced. Stories are sometimes relayed as the facts with little or no facial expression or indication of feeling, depending on the person's relationship to the experience.

Different ways of expressing feelings are also related to an individual's orientation to his or her perception of the self. That is, individuals who tend to view themselves as independent actors may be more inclined to exhibit their emotions more visually and vocally as a means to create an effect on others or to influence their contexts to mirror their own experiences (Heine, Lehman, Markus, & Kitayama, 1999; Morling, Kitayama, & Miyamoto, 2002; Weisz, Rothbaum, & Blackburn, 1984). In contrast, individuals who tend to view themselves as more interdependent with others may be more inclined to be subtle with their feelings or quell their emotions as a way to fit in with others (Heine, Lehman, Markus, & Kitayama, 1999; Morling, Kitayama, & Miyamoto, 2002; Weisz, Rothbaum, & Blackburn, 1984). For example, an individual who wins a contest or game and has a more interdependent view of the self may temper her expression of success in order to reduce potential jealousy or hurt feelings of those who did not win, as compared to those who have a more independent self-perception (Miyamoto, Uchida, & Ellsworth, 2010).

Another factor that influences the expression of emotion is related to the tendency for some people to feel comfortable experiencing stimulating positive emotions such as exhilaration, elation, or delight as compared to some people who have a tendency to feel more comfortable experiencing mellower positive emotions such as serenity, tranquility, or calmness (Tsai, Knutson, & Fung, 2006; Tsai, Louie, Chen, & Uchida, 2007). This can account for different visual and vocal responses to the same positive event: The individual who tends toward comfort with stimulating emotions might jump up and down with a large smile on her face, and the person who tends toward more comfort with mellower emotions might appear placid with a smile on his face. Each of these people may evaluate or read the other with disdain. For example, the person who feels more comfortable with the mellower emotions may think the person jumping up and down is "over the top" and feel that she just wants to be a big shot or to even make others jealous. In contrast, the person who feels more at home with the stimulating emotions may think that the calm body language suggests the mellow person is aloof, cold, or even entitled. In summary, uncovering a client's emotions and reflecting feelings is a challenge; or, as I noted in a previous chapter, clinical practice is "rocket science." In the next section I present some strategies for applying this skill.

BUILDING THE SKILL FOR REFLECTING FEELINGS

The first step to gaining skills for reflecting feelings is to do your own feeling inventory. How many emotion words can you list off the top of your head? What is your first memory of seeing someone cry, express anger, or joy? What is your first memory of expressing your feelings, and how did those around you react? Does that reaction influence how you express those feelings today? Do you assess your expression of feelings as being more aligned with an independent self-perception or interdependent self-perception? How might these experiences influence the way you respond and react to the feelings clients share?

Skills Practice—Reflecting Emotions: Part 1

- Read the following clinical interview, which was also presented in Chapter 2, in which a practitioner uses self-disclosure in a way that is not helpful for the client.
- Underline all of the feeling words that the client and the interviewer use and also write out other feeling words that could be related to each of the words you underline. Then talk with a classmate or colleague if the other feeling words you came up with suggest a more stimulating feeling or a mellow sentiment. For example, in the opening of the interview the clinician states he is "glad" the client could get out of study hall that day for a session. Other feeling words associated with feeling glad include happy, thrilled, joyful, relieved, content, grateful, and pleased. Although "thrilled" is a more stimulating feeling compared to glad, "pleased" is a mellower feeling compared to glad. Now, in collaboration with your classmate or colleague discuss how a client who is more comfortable with stimulating feelings might react to the

interviewer using these various feeling words as compared to a client who is more comfortable with mellower feelings. Then discuss how your choice of feeling words during a session might influence the kinds of clients you serve in your internship or work.

- Re-create the interview dialogue so that the interviewer reflects each of the client's feeling statements in a way that allows the client to hear what he is saying, but not in a way that makes the client feel as if a parrot is in the room. For example, the second statement that the client makes is, "Yeah, it sucks." Although "it sucks" is not an official emotion word that you would find on any feelings charts, it does communicate a feeling. As such, reflecting that feeling might be done in the following ways: "Sounds like it's pretty miserable." "Yeah, that is so unsettling." Now review the new feeling words you came up with and decide if you tended to use feeling words that were more stimulating than the words the client used or if you used feeling words that were mellower than the words the client used or if you used feeling words that were more on par with the level of stimulation or mellowness that the client used. How might the client react to your use of those words to reflect his feelings?

- Now re-create the interview dialogue as if you were the interviewer's supervisor and reflect each of the interviewer's expressed feelings about his parents' divorce. Now review the new feeling words you came up with and decide if you tended to use feeling words that were more stimulating than the words the interviewer used or if you used feeling words that were mellower than the words the interviewer used or if you used feeling words that were more on par with the level of stimulation or mellowness that the interviewer used. How might the interviewer react to your use of those words to reflect his feelings?

The following is an interview dialogue from the first session between a 16-year-old male client, Matt, and a 35-year-old male school social worker in which Matt shares his concerns about his parents' divorce (McKenzie, 2011, pp. 308–310; McKenzie & Nicotera, in press).

INTERVIEWER: Hi, Matt. I'm glad you could get out of study hall and see me today.

MATT: No problem, I really wanted to come to see you.

INTERVIEWER: So, I understand that your parents are going through a divorce.

MATT: Yeah, it really sucks.

INTERVIEWER: Well, you know my parents divorced when I was your age, and I really had a hard time with it, too. I know what you're going through.

MATT: Yeah, what was your parents' divorce like?

INTERVIEWER: My dad was an alcoholic, and my mom couldn't take it any more so she started having an affair with one of our neighbors down the street. It was very awkward.

MATT: Boy, that must have been a pretty tough thing. How did you handle it?

INTERVIEWER: Well, I needed to get away from all of the craziness, so I started using drugs and drinking.

MATT: Did your parents find out about it?

INTERVIEWER: Eventually they did. They made me go to drug rehab. That was really intense and I hated it at the time, but when I think about it now, it might have been the best thing.

MATT: Well, my situation doesn't seem like it is anything as bad as yours. Maybe I should just suck it up and deal with it.

INTERVIEWER: Everybody's life is different, Matt. Let's talk about your situation.

MATT: My folks just told me last week that they were getting a divorce. I didn't see it coming; I thought they were getting along.

INTERVIEWER: Yeah, with my parents I wasn't a bit surprised. I just had a hard time being in the middle of it. You know, my mom wanted to talk about my dad, and my dad after he had been drinking would start crying with me about my mom. It was really tough.

MATT: Like I said, my situation doesn't seem anywhere near as bad as yours.

INTERVIEWER: Well, maybe not, Matt, but tell me how you're feeling about it.

MATT: I'm confused right now, and sort of angry I think, but I'm not sure why.

INTERVIEWER: I got real angry with my folks. I thought they were both acting kind of immature. Do you feel that way about your parents?

MATT: Like I said before, I'm not exactly sure how I feel, but I knew I needed to talk to someone about it. That's why I came to see you.

INTERVIEWER: Well, I'm glad you did, Matt. Talking these things out can be really helpful.

MATT: I hope so.

INTERVIEWER: Sure, it will. Let's meet again tomorrow to talk about it some more.

MATT: OK. But what should I do about how I'm feeling?

INTERVIEWER: Well, you know that I just used drugs to get away from the feelings. I wouldn't suggest that.

Skills Practice—Reflecting Emotions: Part 2

- Work with another classmate or colleague and take turns creating an audiovisual recording of you interviewing each other about the list of questions noted earlier that address experiences with emotion. Be your real selves. Do not make up a therapy problem or setting. If you do not have access to audiovisual recording, then work in teams of three classmates or colleagues and take turns being the observer to complete the next step.

- When you are interviewing your colleague or classmate, listen carefully for the emotions he or she expresses when telling the own story of how he or she learned about feelings. Reflect the emotions that your interviewee shares as a way to explore if you clearly understand his or her experiences. For example, if your interviewee tells a story about being silenced for sharing her anger when she was a child, then you might reflect back to her in one of the following ways, depending on the story she tells: "It sounds like being told to be quiet and not be angry only made you feel more anger." "I hear you, after that you might have been angry and also felt ashamed." "What happens when you get angry now?"

- After you complete your role as the interviewer, watch it with the classmate or colleague you interviewed. Ask the person you interviewed to give you feedback on how you reflected his or her feelings during the interview. For example, did your interviewee feel you matched his or her feeling content or did your interviewee experience your reflection of his or her feelings as misaligned with what his or her actual emotions were during the interview? Then switch roles and do the same thing for the person who interviewed you.

ELICITING MEANING

Uncovering the meanings that clients make out of their situation is as important and complex as reflecting their feelings. It is the meaning we make out of what we experience that has a lasting impact on us, because we are likely to become the stories we tell ourselves about ourselves, others, and events in our lives. Meaning is an important component of clinical intervention modalities such as narrative therapy (White, 2007; White & Epston, 1990) and cognitive-behavioral therapy (Beck, 1979, 2011).

This section of the chapter describes basic skills for uncovering the meanings that clients make to explain their lives to you and themselves. As clinical interviewers, we need to be consistently aware that the meanings clients make are personal and must come from them, not from us. In addition, what something means to a client is embedded in the client's cultural, ethnic, spiritual selves. We cannot assume to know what a client means and must use the basic skills from other chapters in this book, such as effective questions and attending, to learn how a client makes meaning.

The following are effective questions for helping a client to explore meaning: What does it mean to you? What sense do you make out of it? What do you think you value about that? What about that is important to you? What do you mean by _____? Tell me the story of (some critical life event). What does each choice mean to you? (Evan, Hearn, Uhlemann, & Ivey, 2011). For example, in the previous interview example with the teenager, Matt, whose parents are getting a divorce, he states, "Well, my situation doesn't seem like it is anything as bad as yours. Maybe I should just suck it up and deal with it" (McKenzie, 2011, p. 309; McKenzie & Nicotera, in press). An interviewer listening to this statement cannot assume to know what Matt means by his situation not being as bad as the interviewer's or about his parents getting a divorce, so we must find a way to ask. The meaning Matt creates around the story of his parents getting a divorce will be built from what Matt values or is important to him about his current life with his parents, among other things. To access Matt's meaning making about his situation, the interviewer might ask, "What important things will be different for you when your parents get divorced?" Matt's response to this question will give clues to what he values about his life as it is with his parents before the divorce. These clues become possible implications for your work with Matt. For example, Matt might share that his life will be different because of some daily interaction he has with his father that will cease when he no longer lives consistently in the same house with him. As clinical interviewers, we also cannot assume that we know what Matt means by "just suck it up and deal with it." In this instance, asking the simple question, "What do you mean by sucking it up and dealing with it?" could help to uncover more about what Matt means. Knowing what he means by this has important clinical implications about how Matt copes with difficult events in his life. Thus, eliciting meaning from a client not only deepens the story; it can also provide inroads to creating goals for change.

Skills Practice—Meaning Making and Identity

- Watch the following Ted Talk titled, "How the worst moments of our lives make us who we are," by following the link provided or by typing the title of the Ted Talk into your Web browser and including the words "Ted Talk" with the title. https://www.ted.com/talks/andrew_solomon_how_the_worst_moments_in_our_lives_make_us_who_we_are

- As you watch the Ted Talk, reflect on how the people the speaker describes, including himself, made meaning out of their experiences. Based on the examples the speaker gives, what story or meaning did each person give to his or her experiences? What difference did the meaning they made or story they told themselves about their experience make for their lives? What story of adversity do you have about yourself and what meaning do you make out of it? How has this impacted who you are today? How have you forged meaning in your life?

- Make a list of the questions you would ask the speaker in the Ted Talk to find out more about the meanings he made out of the different adversities he faced. Why would you use those questions?

Skills Practice—Uncovering Meaning

- Work with another classmate or colleague and take turns creating an audio-visual recording of you interviewing each other about a difficult life experience you had but that is resolved for you. Be your real selves. Do not make up a therapy problem or setting. If you do not have access to audiovisual recording, then work in teams of three classmates or colleagues and take turns being the observer to complete the next step.
- When you are interviewing your colleague or classmate, intentionally strive to uncover the meaning he or she made out of the experience. Use the questions suggested earlier to gather insights into the meaning or values your colleague placed on his or her experience.
- After you complete your role as the interviewer, watch it with your interviewee. Pick out the spots in the interview where you feel that you learned about the deeper meanings from your interviewee. Stop the recording there and ask your interviewee to give you feedback on that moment in the interview. What happened for the interviewee? How did your question or comment affect him or her and the story he or she was telling? Then switch roles and do the same thing for the person who interviewed you.
- Now have a conversation with your interviewee to discuss the role of the clinical interviewer in assisting clients to uncover the meanings or stories they tell themselves about the problems they experience.

CHALLENGING INCONGRUITY

The clinical interviewing skill of challenging incongruity involves assisting clients in uncovering the disparate or contradictory ways they think about their concerns and the stories they tell themselves about their concerns. Putting this skill into action requires three important steps. The first step requires clinicians to explore and be aware of their own contradictions and the way they use them to rationalize ways of being or thinking that in the end may not be very helpful for their own well-being or core beliefs. This step is the key to successful implementation of the other steps because seeing this in yourself deepens your empathy and compassion for clients and their incongruities. It sets the stage for you being able to challenge clients' incongruities in a nonjudgmental manner that communicates unconditional positive regard.

The second step requires you to develop a special kind of listening for the discrepancies that arise in a client's narrative. When you hear an incongruity in your client's story, then you must decide if it is something that needs to be addressed and if the time is right for challenging it. Becoming more attuned to your own discrepancies allows you to hear them in others and consider if they ought to be addressed as you try on when and why you would accept someone challenging you on a discrepancy. It is helpful to review some of the more common or obvious incongruities as means to developing your self-awareness and listening for them in narratives. Some of the most obvious incongruities occur in the days after people make New Year's resolutions. For example, someone makes a New Year's resolution to eat more fresh vegetables to increase his health. However, after the first few days he decides he is too busy or too tired for all that chopping and forgoes the resolution. He rationalizes the contradiction between keeping and forgoing his resolution with the idea that he is too busy or tired, perhaps for important reasons related to work or family. Nonetheless, there is an incongruity between his value for increased health and his actions related to that value (i.e., not actually eating more fresh vegetables). In a clinical sense, if your client shared this contradiction with you, then you would need to decide whether or not to bring it to his attention. If the contradiction does not have adverse effects on the client's life and it is not related to one of the goals he sets for his work with you, then you might simply take note of the incongruence and move on in the session. However, if the client has created a goal to increase healthy habits as a result of his work with you, then it would be important to address it.

The third step involves addressing a client's discrepancy so he can become aware of it. This can be challenging because very few people truly feel comfortable admitting, for example, that their actions do not support their goals or beliefs. Instead, as the earlier example suggests, we often rationalize our incongruities, sweeping them under the rug in order to maintain emotional, cognitive, or moral comfort. However, when a client acknowledges the incongruent nature of his or her thinking, actions, or feelings, then the client can choose to address them, if needed, for making the positive changes he or she seeks. How clients react to being challenged on incongruities depends on how ready they are to hear it and how it is brought to their attention. You cannot control how ready a client is to hear you uncover an incongruence in his or her narrative, but you can practice and gain skills for addressing them with clients.

- Read the following statements that a client might make and type out your responses to the questions that follow the statements or discuss your response with a classmate or colleague who has read the same statements.

Client example 1:

The client has entered a safe home due to intimate partner violence. The client is visibly bruised on her arms and neck and tells you she is afraid of her partner, who has caused the bruises. A few minutes into the clinical interview the client states, "But, really, how can I leave her for good? She really is my soulmate."

Client example 2:

The client is at his third employee assistance counseling session with you. At the initial session, he shared that he had been fired from his last three jobs for not completing tasks on time. Today in this session when you ask how things are going, the client states, "My boss is mad at me again and I may be fired because I was late again and had too much wine at the business lunch. Life would be much better if I was my own boss."

- What are the main elements that suggest the contradiction?
- What is the question you could ask to help the client begin to detect his or her own incongruence?
- What is the reflection-of-feeling statement you could make that might help with challenging the incongruity?
- What can you ask or say to uncover meaning that might help the client to consider his or her values or what is important to him or her and weigh these out as the client works toward resolving the dilemma?
- How would you challenge each of these clients? How would your approach be different with client one compared to client two? Why would you use these different approaches?

- Work with another classmate or colleague and take turns creating an audiovisual recording of you interviewing each other about a current dilemma in your life. Be your real selves. Do not make up a therapy problem or setting. If you do not have access to audiovisual recording, then work in teams of three classmates or colleagues and take turns being the observer to complete the next step.

- When you are interviewing your colleague or classmate, intentionally listen for the incongruence in his or her dilemma. Follow these suggestions as you conduct the interview: (1) listen for main elements that suggest a contradiction or incongruence, (2) pose questions that might help your interviewee to detect his or her own incongruence, (3) use reflection-of-feelings statements that might help the client to detect his or her own incongruity, (4) use the skill of uncovering meaning to help your interviewee explore the values or importance of his or her dilemma.

- After you complete your role as the interviewer, watch it with your interviewee. Pick out the spots in the interview where you feel that you uncovered the contradictions in his or her dilemma. Stop the recording at those spots and ask your interviewee to give you feedback on that moment in the interview. What happened for him or her? How did your question or comment affect the interviewee in discussing and uncovering the discrepancies that his or her dilemma presents. Then switch roles and do the same thing for the person who interviewed you.

WELLNESS EXERCISE

The role of the clinician is to listen for the strengths in clients' stories, even though those stories are typically problem focused and many times include traumatic and/or painful experiences. The content of client stories has an effect on helping professionals, making them more likely to experience high rates of work-related stress and burnout (Azar, 2000; Figley, 1995, 2002). A consistent practice of mindfulness meditation can reduce stress and promote well-being (Goyal, Singh, & Sibinga, 2014; http://www.unh.edu/health-services/ohep/meditation). Focusing the breath is an important component of mindfulness meditation because it can induce the natural calming system of the body and bring a sense of calm during stress (Kabat- Zinn, 2013). An excellent breathing mindfulness mediation can be found on the University of New Hampshire health and counseling website by using the following link and scrolling to Breath Meditation (http://www.unh.edu/health-services/ohep/meditation) or by following this link to the same mediation on YouTube (https://www.youtube.com/watch?v=j7a-2NYUTCQ).

The more you practice awareness of your breath, the more easily you will be able to call on it to calm yourself in stressful moments with a client. Practicing to use the breath may seem like an odd idea since we breathe without thinking about it every second we are alive and, in fact, many of us do not attend to our breath at all until something that keeps us from breathing occurs. Using the breath as a calming activity does not have to be obvious to anyone besides you; hence, you can use your breath when you want to emphasize silence in a session or take a moment to consider how you will respond to a client and his or her story.

In addition to the breath meditation noted earlier, the following exercise (Nicotera, & Laser-Maira, 2016, pp. 68–69), belly breathing, is useful for learning to notice and pay attention to your breath. It is something you can use whenever you want to at any moment without drawing attention to the fact that you are breathing to reduce your stress. Belly breathing is something that infants do naturally when they are content, so if you have the opportunity to watch a content infant, notice how his or her belly raises on the inhale and lowers on the exhale. The following exercise is meant to help you remember how to breathe in this same calming manner.

Step 1: Belly breathing is in itself a simple inhale and exhale process with the added physical dimension of attending to what happens in the belly when one inhales and exhales. If [you are] comfortable it can be easiest to learn belly breathing while lying on one's back . . . [but may also be practiced sitting in a comfortable, upright position]. Many times, we also imagine that the eyes need to be closed for these activities, when in fact, there is no requirement for the eyes to be shut. Rather than shutting the eyes [you can simply] lower [your] gaze to a small area in order to give the brain a chance to become quiet and not be influenced by visual stimuli.

Step 2: Once [you are] settled as discussed above, put [your] hand on [your] belly, right over the navel is a good direction. Now be aware of what happens in the belly when [you inhale and exhale smoothly] . . .. what happens to the belly? Does it rise on the inhale or contract on the inhale? Does it and contract on the exhale or rise on the exhale?

Step 3: The goal is to learn to have the inhale cause the belly to rise and the exhale cause the belly to contract, but not everyone experiences this the first or even tenth time they try to do it. In fact, some people work hard to control the breath and can feel light headed or breathless. [If you experience this, then return to your regular way of breathing and take a break until you feel ready to practice breath awareness again.]

REFERENCES

Azar, S. T. (2000). Preventing burnout in professionals and paraprofessionals who work with child abuse and neglect cases: A cognitive behavioral approach to supervision. *In Session: Psychotherapy in Practice, 56*(5), 643–663.

Beck, A. (1979). *Cognitive behavior therapy and the emotional disorders.* New York, NY: Penguin Books.

Beck, J. (2011). *Cognitive behavior therapy* (2nd ed.). New York, NY: Guilford.

Cummins, L., Sevel, J., & Pedrick, L. (2006). *Social work skills demonstrated.* Boston, MA: Pearson.

Evan, D., Hearn, M., Uhlemann, M., & Ivey, A. (2011, 8th ed.). *Essential interviewing: A programmed approach to effective communication.* Belmont, CA: Thompson Brooks/Cole.

Evans, D. R., Hearn, M. T., Uhlemann, M. R., & Ivey, A. E. (2017). *Essential interviewing: A programmed approach to effective communication.* Boston, MA: Cengage Learning.

Figley, C. R. (Ed.) (1995). *Compassion fatigue: Coping with secondary traumatic stress disorder in those who treat the traumatized.* New York, NY: Brunner/Mazel.

Figley, C. R. (Ed.) (2002). *Treating compassion fatigue.* New York, NY: Routledge.

Goyal, M., Singh, S., Sibinga, E., Gould, N., Rowland-Seymour, A., Sharma, R., … Haythornthwaite, J. (2014). Meditation programs for psychological stress and well-being: A systematic review and meta-analysis. *JAMA Internal Medicine, 174*(3), 357–368. doi:10.1001/jamainternmed.2013.13018

Heine, S. J., Lehman, D, R., Markus, H. R., Kitayama, S. (1999). Is there a universal need for positive self-regard? *Psychological Review, 106*(4), 766–794. http://dx.doi.org/10.1037/0033-295X.106.4.766

Ivey, A. (2007). *Intentional interviewing and counseling: Facilitating client development in a multicultural society.* Belmont, CA: Thomson Brooks/Cole.

Kabat-Zinn, J. (2013). *Full catastrophe: Using the wisdom of your body and mind to face stress, pain, and illness.* New York, NY: Bantam Books.

McKenzie, F. (2011). *Interviewing for the helping professions: A relational approach.* New York, NY: Oxford University Press.

McKenzie, F., & Nicotera, N. (in press). *Interviewing for the helping professions: A relational approach.* New York, NY: Oxford University Press.

Miyamoto, Y., Uchida, Y., & Ellsworth, P. C. (2010). Culture and mixed emotions: Co-occurrence of positive and negative emotions in Japan and the United States. *Emotion, 10*(3), 404–415. http://dx.doi.org/10.1037/a0018430

Morling, B., Kitayama, S., & Miyamoto, Y. (2002). Cultural practices emphasize influence in the United States and adjustment in Japan. *Personality and Social Psychology Bulletin, 28*(3), 311–323.

Nicotera, N., & Laser-Maira, J. (2016). *Innovative skills to support well-being and resiliency in youth.* New York, NY: Oxford University Press.

Rogers, C. (1995). *A way of being.* New York, NY: Houghton Mifflin.

Rogers, C. (2007). The necessary and sufficient conditions of therapeutic personality change. *Psychotherapy: Theory, Research, Practice, Training, 44*(3), 240–248.

Tervalon, M., & Murrau-Garcia, J. (1998). Cultural humility versus cultural competence: A critical distinction defining physician training outcomes in multicultural education. *Journal of Health Care for the Poor and Underserved, 9*(2), 117–125.

Tsai, J. L., Knutson, B., & Fung, H. H. (2006). Cultural variation in affect valuation. *Journal of Personality and Social Psychology, 90*(2), 288.

Tsai, J. L., Louie, J. Y., Chen, E. E., & Uchida, Y. (2007). Learning what feelings to desire: Socialization of ideal affect through children's storybooks. *Personality and Social Psychology Bulletin, 33*(1), 17–30.

Weisz, J., Rothbaum, F., & Blackburn, T. (1984). Standing out and standing in: The psychology of control in America and Japan. *American Psychologist, 39*(9), 955–969. http://dx.doi.org/10.1037/0003-066X.39.9.955

White, M. (2007). *Maps of narrative practice*. New York, NY: Norton.

White, M., & Epston, D. (1990). *Narrative means to therapeutic ends*. New York: Norton.

5

Skills for Understanding the Context of the Client's Story and Creating Goals

---

THIS CHAPTER COVERS interviewing skills for getting to know the client beyond his or her individual experiences. You will learn how to use a tool that helps you and the client assess how contexts, such as the client's family, faith, employment, school, community, society, and culture, and multiple identities with related marginalizing experiences, interact to affect the client's present challenges and support his or her strengths. You will also learn to work with the client to assess his or her readiness for change and skills for working with the client to create goals.

SIX STEPS FOR EXPLORING CHANGE IN CONTEXT

Each client you see in clinical practice will have a list of reasons for and obstacles to change that arise from within the client and from people in the client's life, such as family members, or larger structures, such as a court system. Gaining a sense of this list can help you and the client assess readiness for change. I invite you to engage in a brief self-reflection in order to gain some insights into this experience. Just try the following steps:

1. Think about a change you would like to make in yourself. Perhaps you would like to cut down on smoking or eat less of a certain food. Or perhaps you would like to create a new habit such as going to bed earlier or getting more exercise.

2. Now rate how important making this change is to you on a scale, where 1 means it is not very important to you and 5 means it is extremely important to you. Based on this number, how ready do you think you are for making this change?

3. Now note as many reasons as you can think of for why you want to make this change.

4. Now note as many obstacles as you can think of to making this change.

5. Next to each reason and obstacle note the word "me" if the reason or obstacle for making the change arises from you, and note the word "other" if the reason or obstacle for making the change arises from some other person or entity. For example, if you want to eat less of a certain food, such as coffee or sugar, and the reason is because of how it makes you feel (e.g., jittery, anxious, restless), then you would note the word "me" next to it. If one of the reasons for eating less coffee or sugar is that your doctor or dentist or an article you read suggested your physical or oral health will be better if you had less of this food, then you would note the word "other" next to it. If "me" and "other" both apply to a reason or an obstacle, then put both words by it.

6. Now take stock of how many of the reasons and obstacles have "me" next to them, how many of them have "other" next to them, and how many have both words next to them. Based on this count, decide for yourself if (a) the reasons for change come more from you or from others in your life and (b) the obstacles to making the change come more from you or from others. How does this relate to the answer you gave for step two, self-rating on importance of making the change and your readiness to make it?

The preceding six steps may be useful in helping clients uncover their own readiness for change and gaining some perspective on the problem at hand. However, there is more to making change than being ready for it. A person's context also plays a role in the change process. Elements of someone's context can include family, friends, school, work, place of worship, or other systems such as government, courts, racism, or sexism. Consider the following example of a client who is working to recover from depression. The client's work in recovery will be challenged not only by his internal experiences (thoughts, feelings, the stories he tells himself about his life) but also by the context surrounding him. For example, if the client has close friends or family supports with whom he can truly be himself and feel loved and comforted, then this will be helpful, a resource. However, if close friends and family are not supportive, denigrate the client's efforts to recover, or even suggest that he ought to just buck up and forget therapy, then they would be viewed as sources of conflict/stress that can impede change. This same client may have a job and coworkers he really enjoys and be motivated to go to work, even on the tough days of feeling depressed. These would be viewed as resources for support that can promote change. Perhaps this client is also an immigrant and experiences microaggressions from daily news stories about government plans to deport those who were not born in the United States, regardless of citizenship status. The news stories and government policy plans represent sources of conflict/stress that can impede change, adding fear to the depression or making him feel unsafe in his own home and community. The client may have close ties with others in their community who immigrated and share the similar fears about the government policy as well as common cultural values. These ties would represent resources for support that can promote change.

There is a formal label and process for depicting a person's context as the previous examples described; it is called the eco-map (Hartman, 1978). An eco-map is a visual representation of an individual and the elements of the context that provide resources for support as well as sources of conflict/stress (see Figure 5.1). The eco-map depicted in Figure 5.1 shows the client mentioned earlier, who is in recovery from depression, and elements of support and conflict/stress. These elements are created in partnership with the client as part of the interviewing process. Straight lines are added between the client and sources of support. Jagged lines are added between the client and sources of conflict/stress. Other types of lines can also be used to depict relationships; some of them mirror the lines used to denote relationships

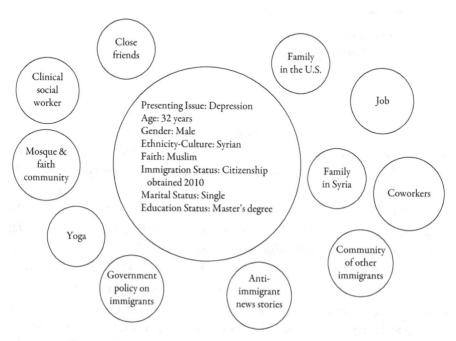

FIGURE 5.1 Elements of an eco-map.

in genograms (McGolderick, Gerson, & Shellengerger, 1999). You and the client can create lines that are specifically meaningful to the client. Just be sure to use a key so that each of you recalls what the lines mean. Look at the eco-map in Figure 5.1 and consider the brief client description from earlier; where would you draw straight lines and where would you draw jagged lines? If you could interview this client, which interviewing skills, from those you have learned thus far, would be most helpful for you to gather the information that will allow you and the client to determine the elements in the eco-map and the type of lines between him and his context?

One way in which you could introduce the idea of creating an eco-map the client described is, "Many times people think that their problems are only about what is happening in their head or their heart. In my practice, I believe that how we think and feel play a role, but I also believe that there are other aspects of someone's life that can affect the way they experience problems. I have a tool to help us assess all of these; it is called an eco-map. Would you be willing to create one with me? I will make a copy for you to keep when we are done." Other suggestions for introducing the client to the eco-map tool are noted in the next section as well as a description of questions and statements a clinician could use during the process.

INTRODUCING THE ECO-MAP AND INITIATING THE PROCESS WITH A CLIENT

Because the term "eco-map" is professional jargon that most clients will not be familiar with, then you must find the right words to introduce it to the client, as noted earlier. Another example you might use with the client described earlier is, "In my practice, I like to get to know you and the parts of your life that you see as helpful as you work to become less depressed and the parts of your life that you see as making it difficult for you to become less depressed. One of the ways we can do this is to draw a map of these different parts of your life; then we can each have a copy of it. Would you be willing to do this with me today?" Another approach could be to tell the client, "It's important that you and I get a sense of the things that contribute to you feeling depressed and the resources in your life that may be helpful. I have a basic tool that can help us put those on paper; it's called an eco-map. If we draw this map together, then I will ask you to tell me about the various things in your life, like people and your work or school. Once we finished I will make a copy of it for you to keep, if you would like. Would you be willing to create one of these with me today?"

After the client agrees to create an eco-map with you, you can offer to do the drawing and writing or offer to have the client do it, depending on his or her comfort level and writing ability. Some clinicians simply begin with a blank sheet of paper, whereas others use a sheet of paper that already has circles drawn on it. One limitation of using a fully blank sheet of paper is that a client can feel overwhelmed by it. On the other hand, if the paper you use already has circles on it, then clients can feel pressured to fill in each and every circle or pressured to not add more circles when they may be necessary. I personally like to begin with a blank sheet of paper and say, "Let me show you how we can start and then you can take up the pencil or leave that part to me. We can start with you here in the center. What are some of the things you think are your strengths, that help you managing your feelings of sadness?" Note, that I would begin with strengths by asking what the client has been doing to manage the depression. Sometimes clients have a tough time noting their strengths, especially people who experience depression; therefore, instead of asking them directly to list strengths, you could ask them to think of someone who knows them well and describe what that person would say are their strengths. Next, I might ask, "What are the ways that you think you might make your life tougher as you deal with the depression?" "What would that same person say are the ways you make your life tougher?" From here I would move to other people in the client's life by asking, "Who comes to mind first when you think of the people in your life? What is your relationship like or how do you get along with that person?" I would keep asking about other people. If the client kept describing only people he or she had conflict with, then I would ask about people with whom the client feels comfort and vice versa. I would also ask about things in the client's life besides people, such as faith, work, and school. I would also ask about elements beyond the person and the typical contexts that he or she might consider, such as the role of music, arts, and sport, in the client's life.

I would want to know if there are any things happening in the community that feel supportive or unsupportive to the client. I would also want to know about any experiences related to sexism, racism, transphobia, or other identity-related oppressive experiences. Many clinicians are leery of posing questions about experiences of microaggressions or direct discrimination, but posing them is essential. Even with clients whose stories or narratives may not obviously "warrant assumptions that race or race-related discrimination may be present, these issues are so subtle, hidden, and omitted in discussions with members from the 'mainstream' that they may be missed in clinical practice unless specifically attended to by the clinician" (Maiter, 2009, p. 273). The same is true for issues of sexism, transphobia, homophobia, classism, ageism, and Islamaphobia, among others. Thus, it is essential to raise questions about experiences of discrimination when a client may have experienced or be currently experiencing the negative effects of these oppressions in his or her life. In the case example presented here, I would ask how he has been coping with the recent government policies aimed at keeping people from Syria out of the United States. However, it may not always be this clear cut, and therefore you will need to ask more directly about racism or transphobia, for example. Fear not, the African American client or transgender client, for example, knows that these oppressions exist and likely experiences microaggressions on a regular basis, so it would be odder to the client if the clinician did not pose questions about it than if the clinician asked about it.

Straightforward questions to a client of color might be, "I know that racism is everywhere, even though many people like to think it doesn't happen anymore and I am wondering how it may be affecting you?" You can switch out the word "racism" for other oppressions depending on how the client identifies. Keep in mind that not all clients will be comfortable sharing these details with you; as noted previously, this kind of information may be communicated very subtly or even hidden from clinicians that the client views as part of a dominant, oppressive group. Not all social, cultural, ethnic, or faith identities are visually evident. However, clinicians who assume a particular identity based on visual appearances could also be completely wrong. Therefore, the clinician needs to listen keenly and also be willing to ask a client about how he or she identifies and not assume anything. For example, when doing the eco-map, the clinician could ask, "Do you have any faith or spiritual practices that are important to you?" In the same vein, you can ask, "In your family did you grow up in any particular faith or spirituality?" You can explore culture and ethnicity by posing questions about family traditions, such as, "Are there family traditions that you find helpful, unhelpful?" Or "Are there family or community traditions you grew up with that you still practice today?" Asking about the past is as important as asking about the present. For example, gay, lesbian, bisexual, or transgender clients may have been raised in families where they were exposed to a great deal of homophobia or transphobia. Some may have been raised in families who tried to use religion or other entities to change their sexual orientation or gender affiliation. In a similar vein, some immigrants may have felt pressured to renounce their cultural, faith, or spiritual practices in favor of a particular faith associated with a religious organization that supported their immigration. These would constitute bitter and painful experiences for which the eco-map can account and, in fact, such experience can and does contribute to depression or other mental health issues. Although faith and spirituality can be resources for well-being, in some cases, these are sources of stress/conflict and extremely damaging experiences. The eco-map is a tool that can help to decipher these experiences, positive and/or negative, that are so important for healing and recovery.

Skills Practice—Creating an Eco-Map

- First, work alone to respond to the six steps for assessing readiness for change noted earlier in this chapter and to create an eco-map of the resources for supporting that change and the stress/conflicts that are obstacles to making the change. Then set this aside and *do not* show your classmate or colleague who works with you in the next parts of this skills practice. That way, when you have completed the following interviewing steps, you and your interviewee can compare how well you did by seeing the number of matches and mismatches between the eco-map you made for yourself and the one made during the interview.

- Work with a classmate or colleague and take turns creating an audiovisual recording of you interviewing each other to (1) gather the information for the six steps for assessing readiness for change noted earlier in this chapter and (2) create an eco-map of the resources for supporting that change and the stress/conflicts that are obstacles to making the change. Be your real selves. Do not make up a therapy problem or setting. If you do not have access to audiovisual recording, then work in teams of three classmates or colleagues and take turns being the observer to complete the next step.

- Begin the interview by introducing your interviewee to the eco-map tool as if he or she had never heard of it. Your interviewee should not just create the eco-map for you. He or she should challenge you to use the clinical interviewing skills you have been learning to gather all the details and engage the interviewee in the process.

- Be sure to practice gathering details on the influence of social structures, policies, and other entities beyond the typical ones such as work, school, family, or faith.

- When the interview is completed, ask your interviewee to show you the eco-map he or she made and assess your use of the skills by comparing how well the eco-map you made during the interview matches the one the interviewee made independently for himself or herself.

- Now watch the audiovisual recording of you interviewing your classmate or colleague. As you watch it, do the following: (1) make a note of each of the different types of interviewing skills you used (e.g., challenging incongruity, reflecting feelings, paraphrases, open and closed questions etc.) and (2) find five places during the interview where you felt you could have done a better job and type out what you would have said or done to make it better.

ASSESSING READINESS FOR CHANGE

There is a useful, formal model that can further your understanding of the change process beyond the readiness for change assessment steps described earlier in this chapter. Although the model, typically referred to as the transtheoretical model of change, was developed for addictions counseling, the model's usefulness reaches beyond addictions work (Prochaska, DiClemente, & Norcross, 1992). The evidence-based model describes five phases of the change process that were developed from research studies on people attempting to make changes in an additive behavior who were in therapy and on those who were trying to make changes on their own (Prochaska et al., 1992). Prochaska and colleagues (1992) note that while the model appears to move from step to step, it does not suggest a neat linear movement from start to finish. Instead, Prochaska et al. (1992) use their research on the model to suggest a "spiral pattern of change" (p. 1104) in which people mostly move back and forth between the phases of change. This is common in recovery from addictions for which the model was developed. However, we can conjecture from this model that the nonlinear flow of behavior change is common to many types of change that a client may want to make, such as leaving a violent partner, rejecting gang membership, or recovery from depression or anxiety. Each of the stages is describe next.

Precontemplation is viewed as an initial phase during which people do not view themselves as having a problem; they do not have an intention to make a change. In their research, Prochaska and colleagues found that research participants who did not have an intention of making change in the next 6 months were in the precontemplation phase. The scholars note that people in this phase may wish to change, but they do not have any intention to change (Prochaska et al., 1992). If you see such individuals in your clinical practice, they will likely tell you that they have come to see you because someone else, such as an employer or spouse, has told them they need counseling. If you use the six steps of readiness for change, they will likely list "other" next to all the reasons for change and will not view any obstacle to making change because they do not believe they need to change.

Contemplation is described as the phase in which "people are aware that a problem exists and are seriously thinking of overcoming it, but have not yet made a commitment to take action" (Prochaska et al., 1992, p. 1103). Individuals in this phase may likely be weighing the pros and cons of making a change, what the personal and social costs would be to making a change (Prochaska et al., 1992). In their research on the model, Prochaska and colleagues (1992) found that individuals contemplating smoking cessation could be in precontemplation for as long as 2 years.

Preparation is the third phase in the model and the research found that people in this phase indicated that they had made a minor change already but have not fully committed to change (Prochaska et al., 1992). "Individuals in this stage are intending to take action in the next month and have unsuccessfully taken action in the past year (Prochaska et al., 1992, p. 1104). An example of this that is beyond issues with addiction is the person who escaped intimate partner violence a couple of times during the past year but returned to the violent partner each time who now comes to a safe home with a stronger intention and perhaps economic or social capacity to stay away this time.

Action is the phase in which the "magic happens." In reality there is no magic involved, but the moments grow and occur in which the person makes real changes needed for lasting recovery. "Action involves the most overt behavioral changes and requires considerable commitment of time and energy" (Prochaska et al., 1992, p. 1104). During the action phase, the client is actively making change toward meeting his or her goals for counseling. Prochaska and colleagues caution that practitioners and clients alike sometimes incorrectly view these actions as actual change, and this is a danger because then the plans for maintaining the new behaviors are not created.

Maintenance is the fifth phase of the model. It is a dynamic process and not a pinnacle one climbs to and then sits on (Prochaska et al., 1992). It involves continual renewal and change efforts to maintain the behavior changes. Prochaska and colleagues characterize individuals in this phase with the following statements: "I need a boost right now to help me maintain the changes I've already made" and "I'm here to prevent myself from having a relapse of my problem" (p. 1104).

Skills Practice—Applying the Transtheoretical Model of Change

- Return to watch the audiovisual recording you created for the skills practice in Chapter 4, "Challenging Incongruity: Part 2," when you interviewed a classmate or colleague about a current dilemma.
- While you are watching the recording again, take note of how your interviewee responded during the interview, especially when you challenged him or her on incongruity. As you take note of these responses, review the phases of change in the transtheoretical model of change and use it to assess how the interviewee's responses align with the different phases. Then create your own assessment of how ready that interviewee was to make the changes necessary for resolving his or her dilemma.

CREATING GOALS

Change, even making a small change, is complicated and fraught with intrapersonal, interpersonal, and structural challenges, as the eco-map exercise demonstrates. This makes it imperative that you engage the client in developing specific and measurable goals for change. Engaging the client so that he or she has ownership over the goals is key for success. Amorphous goals such as "I want to be happier" are not helpful, but a client whose goal is to be happier can be coached to create the steps and actions related to that aspiration. If you have been reading and practicing the skills in this book, you will be able to apply them toward helping a client arrive at goals.

The first step in creating goals is understanding what the client wants to be different as a result of spending time with you; for instance, what would make it worth it to them to have spent the effort and energy to meet with you? The eco-map tool is an important precursor to creating goals because it points to what clients may want more or less of in their lives at the intrapersonal, interpersonal, and structural levels. Some clients will have intrapersonal goals for gaining a clearer grasp of their emotional, physical, spiritual, and thinking selves. Other clients may have issues that point to interpersonal goals for developing healthy relationships on various levels from romantic to friendship to collegial. Still other clients' goals may be related to structural concerns such as access to healthcare or basic resources or combatting microaggressions in the workplace or their daily lives. Likely, clients will have goals within these various levels or the goal at one level may require a goal at another level. For example, the client who wants to see a structural change in her life by reporting microaggressive work experiences may need to develop intrapersonal confidence and may also have interpersonal goals related to challenging the microaggressor at work and/or interpersonal goals for bringing her report through the various human resources components of her workplace.

There are key questions related to intrapersonal change and goals: How will you be different when we are done with counseling? What will you be saying differently, what will you be thinking differently, and what will you be feeling differently? What kind of story will you be telling yourself? Key questions toward interpersonal change and goals include the following: What will others notice about you that will let us know we no longer need to meet? What will you be able to do in relationship to peers, coworkers, bosses, and so on that will let you know it is time to be done with counseling? Key questions for creating goals related to structural changes include the following: How will your day at work feel different when we are done with counseling? What will be different about how you react to microaggressions when we have completed counseling? Who will know about this discrimination issue at work as a result of our working together?

Whatever levels the client's goal fall within, it helps to try and begin each goal with the words "Client will be able to . . ." as this is an active stance and engages the client as the main change agent in his or her own life. Clients often have big goals and your role is to assist them in breaking those big goals into smaller steps, encouraging them to attempt small changes first that will likely lead to success and build confidence for larger changes to come. Remember that goals are equally about changes that remove something, such as a particular behavior or damaging story clients tells themselves, as they are about changes that promote or grow a behavior or new story to tell themselves. For example, when I was in clinical social work practice, I worked with children and their families and the focus was often on what adults in the family wanted a child to stop doing. My role was to assist the family and child to envision what it would be like in the absence of that behavior they wanted the child to stop. In other words, the parent might want the child to stop talking back when asked to do chores, and I would attempt to have the parent and child envision what actions would replace talking back; that is, what were we going to work on together that the child could use instead of talking back? Reading this may make that process seem simple, but it is actually quite complex because when a negative intrapersonal, interpersonal, or structural issue has been occurring for a long time, thinking of the positive replacement for omitting the negative is no small task. In more simple language, when one has a headache or a toothache, the goal is to eliminate it, but the bigger challenge is naming the experience of the absence of the pain—how will you feel and think when that pain is gone? This kind of goal setting causes you and the client to think in terms of possibilities and strengths that can lead to lasting change.

Skills Practice—Creating Goals

- Work with the same classmate or colleague you worked with to create the audiovisual recording of you interviewing each other to (1) gather the information for the six steps for assessing readiness for change noted earlier in this chapter and (2) create an eco-map of the resources for supporting that change and obstacles to obtaining that change.
- Continue the interview as if it were the next session after completing the eco-map and use your interviewing skills to engage your interviewee in creating three specific and measurable goals toward making the change he or she identified during the eco-map interview. Do your best to help your interviewee create goals about what will be, as opposed to what will be gone or eliminated. Base the goals on strengths. When you are the interviewee, challenge your classmate or colleague to work at engaging you; make it tough on your classmate so he or she gets the most out of this practice.
- After the goals are created, talk with your classmate or colleague and decide if the goals fall within the intrapersonal, interpersonal, or structural level of change or some combination. In this discussion decide if the entire change the interviewee wants can be made by working from only one of the levels or if the interviewee needs to focus on more than one level and consider why this is or is not so for that person.

WELLNESS EXERCISE

The following wellness activity combines mindfulness meditation with the physical activity of walking or rolling. Typically, this is called a walking meditation; however, some people roll instead of walk, so this exercise is described for both. "The way we typically walk [or roll] is goal-directed, sometimes it is hurried and often we are so lost in thoughts of where we are headed or what we will do when we arrive that we miss the present moment of the walking itself. Walking [or rolling] meditation is a complete contrast to this kind of goal-directed walking and involves walking [or rolling] in silence, conscious of your footsteps [the movement of your arms, the sound of your wheels] and your breath without changing or judging them. Naturally, your eyes are open, so you can see, but your gaze is calm and inward" (Nicotera & Laser-Maira, 2016, p. 85). You can try the following steps to practice a walking or rolling meditation or type the words *walking meditation* into your Web browser for numerous examples of walking meditations (e.g., https://www.youtube.com/watch?v=tUWMrKZ9VSU; https://www.youtube.com/watch?v=nYO7kedlfYw).

Step 1: Begin this activity either inside or outside in a comfortable, open space that is free of obstacles that inhibit movement. Decide how long you want to practice this meditation and set your mobile phone or watch timer for that many minutes (a minimum of 10 minutes is recommended). Take a moment to draw in an awareness of where you are; what is around you, what do you see, hear, feel, smell? Now slowly inhale and exhale several times and notice your internal state. How are you at this moment? How do you sense your breathing, your heart beating, your thoughts?

Step 2: Now begin to roll or walk and notice the sound that this makes, notice the movement of your arms as you roll your chair or walk, notice the feel of the ground beneath you; how does it sound, how does it feel as you walk or roll over it? Remind yourself that you have nowhere to be and nothing to do, except to be where you are at this moment.

Step 3: As you roll or walk, return to your breath. What has happened to it while you were focused on other things? Bring it back to slow inhales and exhales. Now notice what is around you; what do you see, hear, and feel that you have not noticed before about this space?

Step 4: As you roll or walk, notice your thoughts; where are they focused—on what you have to do next or what happened yesterday? Bring your thoughts to the present moment, and be grateful that you are making this time to take care of yourself.

Step 5: Begin to finished this moving meditation by refocusing your breath and thoughts in the present moment and then stop walking or rolling. Look around you; take in what you see, hear, and feel. Breath in slowly and exhale slowly before ending this meditation.

REFERENCES

Hartman, A. (1978). Diagrammatic assessment of family relationships. *Social Casework*, October, 465–476.

Maiter, S. (2009). Using an anti-racist framework for assessment and intervention in clinical practice with families from diverse ethno-racial backgrounds. *Clinical Social Work Journal*, *37*, 267–276.

McGolderick, M., Gerson, R., & Shellengerger, S. (1999). *Genograms: Assessment and intervention*. New York, NY: Norton.

Nicotera, N., & Laser-Maira, J. (2016). *Innovative skills to support well-being and resiliency in youth*. New York, NY: Oxford University Press.

Prochaska, J., DiClemente, C., & Norcross, J. (1992). In search of how people change: Applications to addictive behaviors. *American Psychologist, 47*(9), 1102–1114.

6

Beginning Skills for Intervention

A COMMON STRUGGLE for clinical interviewers-in-training or those who are newly trained is delaying their desire to "fix" or make things better for the client before the whole story has unfolded. Attempts to "fix" a client or to make his or her problems go away typically come off as advice giving, such as "Have you tried . . . ?" or "What if you . . . ?" These well-intentioned attempts often frustrate clients who have likely tried many things to make their situation better before making the appointment for formal counseling. This chapter covers some basic interviewing skills that new clinical interviewers can use, after they have a good sense of the client's story, to launch the change or intervention process with clients. The skills are drawn from solution-focused therapy (De Jong & Kim Berg, 2008; DeShazer, 2000), and the empty chair technique is drawn from gestalt therapy (Kellogg, 2004, 2007; Paivio & Greenberg, 1995; Perls, 1973, 1975). Describing the whole of each of these interventions and related theories is beyond the scope of this essential interviewing skills book. Therefore, a list of readings for further information is provided at the end of this chapter. The skills covered here are basic entry-level skills related to these practice interventions and readers should obtain further training in each of them before declaring themselves fully trained.

SOLUTION-FOCUSED SKILLS

Solution-focused therapy was codeveloped by two clinical social workers, Insoo Kim Berg and her colleague, Steve de Shazer. They practice together at the Brief Family

Therapy Center in Wisconsin, where Ms. Kim Berg was the Center director and Mr. De Shazer was the research director. Their ideas for solution-focused therapy were founded after years of listening to clients and realizing that while clients wanted solutions, therapists were focused on problems to the point of getting stuck in a problem mentality that made finding solutions difficult at best, if not impossible (Kim Berg, 2010). Through reflecting on their own clinical practices and observing the students they were training, Kim Berg and De Shazer noted the deficits in the traditional medical model of problem-focused treatment that applied questions aimed at (1) uncovering the problem, (2) sorting out mistakes the client made that contributed to it, (3) getting a deeper sense of causes from the client's past that contributed to the problem, (4) asking the client to share his or her feelings about the problem, and (5) suggesting what the client could do to "fix" the problem, such as "Have you ever tried . . . ?"

Kim Berg and De Shazer turned this problem-focused medical model on its head to develop the solution-focused model, which views clients as the experts in their lives as well as the holders of strengths and solutions to their concerns. The clinical interview begins similarly to learn about the client's concerns; however, the clinician holds a stance of *curious listening* as the client responds to an initial question of "How can I be useful to you?" or "When you look back on the time you spent with me, what will be the one thing that will make you say it was worth it to spend that time in therapy?" Although these questions typically set the client up to describe the problem, they also focus on outcomes from the beginning of the process by asking about what will be different (De Jong & Kim Berg, 2008).

The solution-focused approach treats *clients as the experts* in their own lives and builds on three aspects of clients as experts. The first aspect engages the client in describing "what they would like to see changed in their lives" (Kim Berg, 2008, p. 19). As De Jong and Kim Berg (2008) note, this initial question to the client does encourage the client to describe the problem that brought him or her into therapy. Even though solution-focused therapy is not problem oriented, the clinician listens carefully to how the client describes the problem but does not encourage a lot of problem talk by asking questions about what might have caused the problem or trying to assign blame for the problem's existence. Instead, the clinician employs questions about how the client has been coping up till now and what it is like on days when there is less of the problem. Such questions might include: "That sounds difficult, how have you managed all of this up till now?" or "What have you been doing to manage (cope with) this each day?" "Is the problem the same each day or does it get better on some days? What are you doing on days when the problem bothers you less?" This line of questioning is meant to encourage the client to move toward the second aspect of *client as expert*, which is getting the client to tell the story of what it looks like currently when the problem is less and eventually to describe the imagined story of what it looks like when the problem is solved (De Jong & Kim Berg, 2008).

Client responses to questions aimed at gaining the client's story of what it is like when the client experiences less of the problem will likely hold clues to the client's strengths and solutions he or she is already use to get through each day (Kim Berg, 2008). These questions and this line of discussion with the client are meant to move the session toward the third aspect of *client as expert* in which the clinician works to discover the client's "perceptions of exceptions to their problem" (De Jong & Kim Berg, 2008, p. 19). The clinician stance in all of solution-focused therapy *is not* as expert assessor and diagnostician. Instead, the clinician is "an expert at exploring clients' frames of reference and identifying those perceptions that clients can use to create more satisfying lives" (De Jong & Kim Berg, 2008, p. 19). Several practical questioning skills associated with the solution-focused approach are the scaling question, the exception question, and the miracle question.

Scaling Questions

The scaling question can be used to "help clients to express complex, intuitive observations about their past experiences and estimates of future possibilities" (De Jong & Kim Berg, 2008, p. 106). For example, the practitioner working with a client whose problem involves anxiety or panic might say, I am going to ask you a question, "one which puts things on a scale from 0 to 10, where 0 equals no panicky feelings and 10 equals the worst panicky feelings you have ever experienced. When you think back to the day you made the appointment with me, what number would you give your panicky feelings [wait for client response]? What number would you give those feelings today [wait for client response]" (De Jong & Kim Berg, 2008, p. 107). The client responses to this scaling question provide insight into how variable the panicky feelings are and the responses also allow the practitioner to pose other related questions. For example, if the client responds that the panicky feelings were at a 7 on the day they called for the appointment, the practitioner can ask, "What was happening on that day when they were at a 7?" The client's response provides important information about the context and experiences surrounding the panicky feelings. This response can be followed by another question such as "How do you manage when your panicky feelings are a 7?" as this will start to explore potential solutions of which the client may not be fully cognizant. The practitioner will also use the client's response to the second part of the scaling question to gain a deeper understanding of the client. For example, if the client responds that the panicky feelings today are at 3 on the scale, then the practitioner can ask the client to describe what he or she has been doing to get those feelings from a 7 to a 3 since the client called for the appointment. On the other hand, the client may say that the feelings are at a 10 today (greater than the 7 on the day the client made the appointment). Even though the client indicates that the panicky feelings are worse, the practitioner can gather more details about the client's experience and context of the panicky feelings by asking what has happened that the feelings increased since making the appointment.

Either of the client responses noted in the previous paragraph can be followed by another scaling question that focuses on getting the client to uncover small action steps he or she can take toward a solution or goal (De Jong & Kim Berg, 2008). For example, in the second response earlier, the client indicates that his or her panicky feelings are at a 10 today and the practitioner can follow up by asking, "What can you do that would help you bring it down from a 10 to a 9.5?"

The scaling question can also be used to assess the client's perception of where he or she sits in the context of the problem by posing a question such as "On a scale from 0 through 10, where 0 equals the worst your problems have been and 10 means the problems we have been talking about are solved, where are you today on that scale?" (De Jong & Kim Berg, 2008, p. 15). The scaling question can also be used to assess a client's motivation or hope for making change. For example, the practitioner can say, "I want to ask you another scaling question, this time about how hard you are willing to work on the problem which brought you in. Let's say that 10 means you are willing to do anything to find a solution, and 0 means that you are willing to do nothing—just sit there and wait for something better to happen. How hard, from 0 to 10, are you willing work?" (De Jong & Kim Berg, 2008, p. 109). Clearly there are many more ways that the scaling question can be used and readers are encouraged to explore Insoo Kim Berg's vast body of work, in both written and DVD formats, to gain more insights and skills for using this line of questioning with clients.

Exception Questions

Exception questions are aimed at helping the client to uncover "past experiences in [his or her] life when the problem might reasonably have been expected to occur, but somehow did not" (de Shazer, 1985, as cited in De Jong & Kim Berg, 2008, p. 103). Exceptions assist the client in finding solutions that he or she has already been doing. When the client learns how he or she makes the exceptions happen, then solutions can be built by the client making more of those exceptions happen (De Jong & Kim Berg, 2008). The goal of the exception question is to explore the "who, what, when, and where of exception times" (De Jong & Kim Berg, 2008, p. 103), and the practitioner listens keenly for these exception times and draws the client's attention to them. De Jong and Kim Berg (2008) point out that solution-focused questions do not include "why" because such questions focus the client on ferreting out latent reasons for the problem, which can result in being stuck in a spiral of problem talk at the expense of finding solutions. Also, many clients perceive "why" questions as criticism by the practitioner, and this can create a spiral of defensive responses on the part of the client, which also detracts from finding solutions (De Jong & Kim Berg, 2008).

One way to pose the exception question is as follows: "Have there been times in the past couple of weeks when the problem did not happen or was less severe?" (De Jong & Kim Berg, 2008, p. 103). However, sometimes clients are not able to see exceptions in themselves, so the practitioner must ask them to view an exception through the eyes of a family member or friend (De Jong & Kim Berg, 2008). For example, the client with the panicky feelings noted earlier may have a difficult time calling up an exception to his or her anxiety, but the client may be able to respond to the exception question as stated earlier. In this case, the practitioner might pose the exception question in the following way, "Suppose I asked your best friend whether you had any better days recently. What would your best friend say?" (De Jong & Kim Berg, 2008, p. 103). De Jong and Kim Berg (2008) point out that the practitioner is not looking for the perfect exception but is seeking a smaller level or rate of a problem. De Jong and Kim Berg (2008) provide the example of an exception for a child who usually talks back to a parent when refusing to do the dishes; it may include the child talking back and initially refusing, but then actually stopping the talking back and doing at least some of the dishes. Responses to exception questions can be followed up with the scaling question to build actions that are steps to the solution. For example, the practitioner could ask, "How hopeful are you, on a scale where 0 equals no hope and 10 equals total hope, that you could plan to do [name exception] on purpose?"

Miracle Questions

Similar to the other solution-focused questions, the miracle question arose from Insoo Kim Berg's interactions with a client who suggested that it would take a miracle for changes to occur, but then went on to describe the after-effects of the miracle as a "worthwhile set of goals from her point of view" (De Jong & Kim Berg, 2008, p. 84). De Jong and Kim Berg (2008) note that the miracle question helps clients to focus on opportunities for solutions, to think outside of the problem-box, and to think about what is to come in their lives. Also, similar to the other questioning skills of the solution-focused approach, the miracle question launches a series of other questions as the client responds as opposed to being a single question and response that finds the solution (de Shazer, 2000, http://www.netzwerk-ost. at/publikationen/pdf/miraclequestion.pdf). Insoo Kim Berg's co-creator, Steve de Shazer, describes the following in a four-part series for using the miracle question in one session. Clearly this is meant as a model for acquainting practitioners with the process, and the steps would need to be varied depending on how the client responds. However, the model presented by these four parts outlines the manner in which beginners can practice.

Part One: I have a strange, perhaps unusual question, a question that takes some imagination (pause here) . . . Suppose (pause again) . . . after we finish here you go home tonight, watch TV, do your usual chores, and then go to bed and to sleep (pause) . . . and while you are sleeping a miracle happens (pause) . . . and the problem that brought you here today is solved, just like that! (pause) . . . But this happens while you are sleeping, so you cannot know that it has happened [pause] . . . Once you wake up in the morning, (a) how will you go about discovering that this miracle has happened to you OR (b) how will your best friend know that this miracle happened to you? (pause and wait out the silence, wait out the client for his or her response. In fact, when the client's response is "un-reasonable," in the therapist's view, the most useful response is to continue in silence, which gives the client a chance to "fix" the response to make it more reasonable.)

Part Two: (a) How will your best friend discover that this miracle happened to you? OR (b) How will you discover that this miracle has happened to you?

Part Three: When was the most recent time (perhaps days, hours, weeks) that you can remember when things were sort of like this day after the miracle?

Part Four: On a scale from 0 to 10, with 10 standing for how things are the day after the miracle and 0 standing for how things were the day you called to arrange this appointment, where—between 0 and 10—are you at this point? (pause for response). On the same scale, where would you think your best friend would say you are? (pause for response). On the same scale, where would you say things were when things were sort of like this miracle day?

(deShazer, 2000, http://www.netzwerkost.at/publikationen/pdf/miracle-question.pdf)

De Jong and Kim Berg (2008) provide further details that are helpful for drilling the client responses down to goals. Because clients often share the miracle as the finished product, the practitioner helps them to create smaller components of it, to make for doable action steps toward the miracle or solution. One way to do this is as follows: "Wow! That sounds like a big miracle. What is the first small thing that you would notice that would tell you things were different?" [after the client responds, the next question is posed and possibly posed again and again after each response to help the client move toward the smallest components of the miracle] What else would tell you things are better? (De Jong & Kim Berg, 2008, p. 354). Another line of questioning is used to help the client make the miracle "concrete, behavioral, and specific" [as the practitioner might say]. "You say the miracle is that you'd feel better. When you feel better, what might others notice different about you that would tell them that you feel better?" (De Jong & Kim Berg, 2008, p. 354). This can be followed by "What might you do different when you feel better? What else?" (De Jong & Kim Berg, 2008, p. 354).

De Jong and Kim Berg (2008) also suggest questions to assist the client in initiating "something different or better [such as] You say that the miracle is that you'd weigh 50 pounds less. Ok, what will be different in your life when you lose that first pound? What else?" (p. 354). Similarly, the following question can be posed as a means to having the client figure out what he or she will be doing differently to replace the actions he or she wants to eliminate: "You say that, when the miracle happens, you'll fight less with your kids. What will you be doing instead?" (De Jong & Kim Berg, 2008, p. 354).

The next two suggested questions assist the client in thinking about how others around him or her will notice the change and then how those individuals will behave in reaction to the client's change. De Jong and Kim Berg (2008) suggest this question: "When the miracle happens, what differences will your husband (children, best friend, coworkers, teachers, etc.) notice about you?" and then a follow-up question after the client responds such as "When your husband (children, best friend, coworkers, teachers, etc.) notice _____ (the difference that the client mentions in answering the previous question), what will your husband (they) do differently? What else? And when he (they) does (do) that, what will you do? And when you do that, what else will be different?" (p. 355). As the client responds to this line of questioning, it is possible for the client to begin to build the miracle into more concrete and doable steps. Anticipating how others will react and how they might make those relationships better can also serve as a motivating factor for the change (De Jong & Kim Berg, 2008).

Clients will have different responses to the unusual line of solution-focused questioning. Some clients might complain that this kind of questioning, especially the miracle question, is difficult. In this case, De Jong and Kim Berg (2008) suggest that the practitioner agree with the client and respond with a statement such as "I am asking you some tough questions, take your time" (De Jong & Kim Berg, 2008, p. 355). Other clients may simply say they do not know what miracle or exception could occur or that they may arrive at an unlikely miracle such as winning the lottery

(De Jong & Kim Berg, 2008). These kinds of responses provide an assessment of the client's level of feeling stuck in the problem and the absence of perhaps any sense of hope about what the client could actually do to create a solution. The solution-focused practitioner, however, does not give up when clients respond in this way. De Jong and Kim Berg (2008) point out that when clients do not know, then push a little more and say, "Suppose you did know, what would you say?" [or move into the significant other question by asking,] "Suppose I was to ask your husband (children, best friend etc.), what would he (they) say?" (De Jong & Kim Berg, 2008, p. 355). On the other hand, when clients come up with an unlikely miracle such as winning the lottery, "just agree with them by saying: that would be nice, wouldn't it? [and follow up with] 'What do you think the chances are of that happening?'" (De Jong & Kim Berg, 2008, p. 355).

Skills Practice—Solution-Focused Questioning

- Return to working with the same classmate or colleague with whom you took turns to create the audiovisual recording of you interviewing each other about a current dilemma in your life (see Chapter 4). Conduct a follow-up interview with that same person and apply the solution-focused questioning (scaling, exception, and miracle) as appropriate to assist him or her in finding a solution to the dilemma. As with the initial interview you created in Chapter 4, be your real selves. Do not make up a therapy problem or setting.

- During this interview allow for a break in the role play to stop and examine the solution-focused questions and tips so you can reapply them when you notice you are getting stuck in the problem focus. This is something that you cannot do in a real session, so take advantage of working with a classmate or colleague to brainstorm what direction you can take to remain in the solution-focused approach.

- Create an audiovisual recording of this interview so you can watch it and learn about what you did well and what you would change the next time you used solution-focused questions.

THE EMPTY CHAIR

The empty chair technique is most often associated with gestalt therapy developed by Fritz Perls (1973, 1975). However, Perls (1973) himself noted that the strategy was born out of psychodrama. The empty chair technique engages clients with themselves, their problem, and others in a unique way that allows them to talk to their problem itself and for their problem to talk to them or to bring other individuals into the session for dialogue even when they cannot be present (Paivio & Greenberg, 1995). To be active in such a dialogue, the client sits in one chair and faces another chair that is empty so that the client imagines the part of herself, her problem, or another person in her life (living or passed) as being present in the room, specifically in that chair. In the process, the client might switch chairs in order to engage some other part of herself, her problem, or to hear what she would say, if she walked in the shoes of the person whom she imagines is sitting in the empty chair. Two empty chair approaches are addressed in this section: the empty chair for internal dialogues and the empty chair for external dialogues.

Empty Chair for Internal Dialogues and External Dialogues

Clients may benefit from the internal dialogue approach if they are wrestling with dilemmas, conflicts, or unhelpful stories they are telling themselves about a problem (Kellogg, 2007). Sometimes the internal dialogue process can lead to the client discovering an inner critic that may have initiated within a relationship with a significant other, such as a parent (Kellogg, 2007). In this case, the practitioner would guide the client toward the external empty chair dialogue. Clients who are struggling with a current or past relationship issue can benefit from the external dialogue approach (Kellogg, 2007). The external empty chair dialogue "engages [the client] in an imaginary dialogue with [a] significant other [and] is designed to access restricted feelings allowing them to run their course and be restructured in the safety of the therapy environment" (Paivio & Greenberg, 1995, p. 419). Paivio and Greenberg (1995) demonstrated the efficacy and lasting effects of this type of empty chair dialogue in a randomized, controlled trial over eight sessions of counseling where the empty chair was the consistent intervention. A full treatment manual for this process is available (Greenberg, Rice, & Elliott, 1993).

Steps in the Empty Chair Process

The setup and process of the empty chair technique are similar, regardless of which approach is used, so the general process is described here. Prior to engaging the client in the empty chair intervention, the first thing that the practitioner does is to help the client bring the concern to the surface of his or her emotions and thoughts. The practitioner encourages the client to speak about the concern from the "I" perspective (Australian Institute of Professional Counselors, 2013). For example, if the client says, "It's frustrating," then the practitioner has the client change the language to "I feel frustrated," in order to engage the client in owning the feeling. Similarly, the practitioner helps the client to be in the present moment with his or her feelings and thoughts versus talking about them as in the past or the future (Australian Institute of Professional Counselors, 2013). For example, if I client says, "I was so confused" about an issue, the practitioner encourages the client to use language about how he or she feels right now. In this case, the clinician may challenge the client by asking, "So you were feeling confused . . . that sounds like the past. What are you feeling right now about this problem?" If the client says, I was so angry with my spouse, then the practitioner issues a similar challenge, but about the spouse as opposed to the feeling; for example, "So you were angry with your spouse last week. What about right now? What are you feeling this moment when you think about this issue with your spouse?"

Once the client has brought his or her emotions and thoughts to the surface and the present, then the practitioner can introduce the empty chair to client and ask if he or she would like to try it (Australian Institute of Professional Counselors, 2013). The practitioner might say, "There is a strategy we can try to see if it will help you to clear up this dilemma or the conflict you are experiencing with your spouse. It involves some imagination and you sitting first in one chair so you can speak directly to the dilemma or your spouse that you imagine is another chair across from you that is empty. It might seem a little odd to you at first, and we can stop it if you feel it isn't right for you, but are you willing try it?" Some clients may need the practitioner to demonstrate the two roles, first sitting in one chair and providing an impersonal example that is not related to the client's issue. When the practitioner is willing to be vulnerable by talking to an empty chair and then switching to the other chair to continue the dialogue, the client can become more comfortable with his or her own vulnerability in doing the same thing.

When the client agrees to try the empty chair approach, ask the client to start off as himself and to name the part of the dilemma that is in the other chair or to imagine his spouse or whomever he needs to have sitting in the empty chair (Australian Institute of Professional Counselors, 2013). Then encourage the client to say whatever comes to him to whomever or whatever is in the chair. This may be a simple, single sentence or a longer monologue, but the initial role of the practitioner is to sit silently and observe. After this initial sentence or longer monologue, ask the client to switch chairs and respond to what he just said as if he were that dilemma or other person (Australian Institute of Professional Counselors, 2013). The process may take several rounds as the client moves back and forth between the chairs to create the dialogue. Once the client has completed some rounds of the empty chair, then the practitioner assists the client in processing the experience; this may include more rounds of empty chair. *The end goal for the empty chair is to assist the client in realizing what he wants, how he can react toward an issue, gain some creative ideas for coping with it, and/or rehearsal of how to interact with someone in his life* (Australian Institute of Professional Counselors, 2013).

Either the internal or the external empty chair dialogue can raise related issues of oppression due to outright discrimination or microaggressions as well as unresolved trauma or loss (Kellogg, 2007). The practitioner should be aware and observant for any of these to arise during this intervention. For example, some clients who have experienced outright discrimination, microaggresssion, or trauma may not be ready to imagine a perpetrator in the chair across from them. The practitioner, in fact, may represent the perpetrator of such experiences and this may cause more stress for the client. Therefore, practitioners who use the empty chair strategy should know their client well as a result of building a strong rapport and trust and using all the other skills from the previous chapters of this book to engage the client in telling his or her story and setting goals for change. When the practitioner has in-depth knowledge of the client and has earned the client's trust, the empty chair can be a powerful ally in assisting the client to work with and through these kinds of experiences.

Skills Practice—Empty Chair

- Return to working with the same classmate or colleague with whom you took turns to create the audiovisual recording of you interviewing each other about a current dilemma in your life (see Chapter 4). Conduct a follow-up interview with that same person and apply the empty chair intervention as appropriate to assist the person in expressing the various sides to the dilemma. As with the initial interview you created in Chapter 4, be your real selves. Do not make up a therapy problem or setting.
- During this interview allow for a break in the role play to stop and examine your use of the empty chair approach so you can restart the process as needed. This is something that you cannot do in a real session, so take advantage of working with a classmate or colleague to brainstorm what direction you can take to remain in the empty chair approach.
- Create an audiovisual recording of this interview so you can watch it and learn about what you did well and what you would change the next time you used the empty chair approach.

WELLNESS EXERCISE

The wellness activity in this chapter is called the "3-minute breathing space mindfulness meditation." It is a common practice taught in mindfulness-based cognitive therapy, which is an evidence-based intervention demonstrating the positive effects on depression and relapse for depression (Segal, Williams, & Teasdale, 2013). It is offered here as a brief wellness exercise that busy practitioners can practice in between meeting with clients. Essentially, the 3-minute breathing space encourages you to set aside 3 minutes to use your breath to find yourself and occupy the space in your body, mind, and heart. Segal, Williams, and Teasdale (2013) refer to this exercise as checking in with the weather pattern in your body by noticing what you are thinking, feeling, and how your body is physically. The following iteration of a 3-minute breathing space is offered as a guide to checking the weather pattern in your body.

To begin, find a quiet, comfortable place where you can sit undisturbed for 3 minutes. Before you set your timer, be sure that your mobile phone and other electronic reminders are silenced. Now start your time and begin. Sit in an aware and relaxed way so that your head is gently lifted toward the sky, your shoulders are gently draping toward your hips, and your feet are gently planted toward the earth. Move through the following sequence without judgement. First, inhale and exhale as you would without thinking about it. As you do this, become aware of your body and notice how it feels. Inhale and exhale and just be aware of how your body feels without changing it or judging it. Next become aware of your thoughts as you inhale and exhale, bringing your thoughts to the present moment and reminding yourself that at this moment there is nothing to do but inhale and exhale. Now shift your awareness to your feelings; you might name them if you are aware of a name for them, or you might feel them somewhere in your body or both. As you inhale and exhale, just be aware of your feelings, without judging them. Now ask yourself, "What is my weather pattern just now, in this moment?" Just notice, but do not try to change it or get rid of it or hold on to it. Now focus on your breath; notice how it feels when you inhale; the air might feel cool as it flows in through your nose. Notice how it feels when you exhale; maybe there is a sound as the air leaves your body through your nose. If you begin to think about what you need to be doing or what has happened in the past, notice this and then bring your attention back to your breathing as you inhale and exhale. Next, use your breath to tune into your body and notice how you are sitting. Has your posture changed since you first started this exercise? What is your facial expression? How are you holding your hands? How does the air feel on your skin? Take this in as it is in this moment and find yourself in your body without judgment. Inhale and exhale several more times with appreciation for what your body, mind, and heart can do.

In addition to the iteration presented here, there are also guided 3-minute breathing space exercises that you can easily locate by typing the words "three minute breathing space" into your Web browser (e.g., https://www.youtube.com/

watch?v=rOne1PoTKL8 or http://www.breathworks-mindfulness.org.uk/3-min-breathing-space or http://www.youtube.com/watch?v=Ula0njZIOh4).

REFERENCES

Australian Institute of Professional Counselors. (2013). *Role play: Gestalt therapy*. Retrieved from https://www.youtube.com/watch?v=AJ4Uyf5X6Sw)

De Jong, P., & Kim Berg, I. (2008). *Interviewing for solutions* (3rd ed.). Belmont, CA: Thompson Brooks/Cole.

de Shazer, S. (1985). *Keys to solution in brief therapy*. New York, NY: WW Norton.

de Shazer, S. (2000). *The miracle question*. Retrieved from http://www.netzwerk-ost.at/publikationen/pdf/miraclequestion.pdf)

Greenberg, L., Rice, L., & Elliott, R. (1993). *Facilitating emotional change: The moment by moment process*. New York, NY: Guilford.

Kellogg, S. (2004). Dialogical encounters: Contemporary perspectives on "chairwork" in psychotherapy. *Psychotherapy: Theory, Research, Practice, Training, 41*(3), 310–320.

Kellogg, S. H. (2007). Transformational chairwork: Five ways of using therapeutic dialogues. *NYSPA Notebook, 19*(4), 8–9. Retrieved from http://transformationalchairwork.com/articles/transformational-chairwork/

Kim Berg, I. (2010). *Irreconcilable differences a solution-focused approach to marital therapy*. San Francisco, CA: Psychotherapy.net.

Paivio, S., & Greenberg, L. (1995). Resolving "unfinished business": Efficacy of experiential therapy using empty chair dialogue. *Journal of Consulting and Clinical Psychology, 63*(3), 419–425.

Perls, F. (1973). *The gestalt approach and eye witness to therapy*. Palo Alto, CA: Science and Behavior Books.

Perls, F. (1975). *Legacy from Fritz*. Palo Alto, CA: Science and Behavior Books.

Segal, Z., Williams, M., & Teasdale, J. (2013). *Mindfulness-based cognitive therapy for depression*. New York, NY: Guilford.

7

Skills for Evaluation and Closure

THIS CHAPTER ADDRESSES skills for closing and evaluating a single session as well as the skills needed to terminate an entire clinical relationship. Closing a session or ending an entire clinical relationship with a client is as important as initiating a session or clinical relationship by building rapport and earning trust. The way in which each session ends can influence the client's experience between sessions. In addition, ending each session with a check-in for the client's experience that day is also integral for communicating the importance of a client's own assessment of the session and that the practitioner welcomes feedback from the client as an expert in his or her own process and life. Ending each session with care is also important because some clients do not return for various reasons and therefore the end of each session could be the last session, even if that is not the intention of the practitioner or client at the time. In the best of all worlds, the ending of the entire clinical relationship is planned and carried out with care. The practitioner approaches this termination with empathy for the ways in which a client may have experienced loss in his or her life, other good-byes, or the absence of a chance to say good-bye in other relationships beyond clinical work.

CLOSING AND EVALUATING A SINGLE SESSION

A general goal for ending a single session could include sending clients off with a reminder of a strength, a sense of hope, or tasks toward meeting an agreed-upon goal for change. In reality, not all sessions will end with a sense of hope or tasks to be completed toward goals because clinical work is messy and making changes in how one feels, thinks, or interacts with the world around oneself cannot always be tied up in a neat bow at the end of every session. Because clinical interviewing is typically about the messy feelings, thoughts, and experiences with which clients struggle, practitioners need to attend the emotional and cognitive state of the client toward the end of each session and work toward helping the client leave the session with some sense of equilibrium, if possible. Sometimes a client will leave a session with feelings of anger, sadness, or grief and this is out of the control of the practitioner. However, working toward sending the client off with a reminder of a strength at the end of each session is a feasible goal. Each of these components of ending a single session is covered next.

Keep Time!

Successfully ending a single session begins with the end of it in mind, which means keeping track of the time. Many new clinical interviewers feel uncomfortable tracking the time in a session for fear that if they check their mobile phone, watch, or a clock during the session, the client will think the practitioner is bored or wanting to rush the process. Keeping track of time does not have to be an imposition on the therapeutic process. One option is to keep a clock in your sight so that you can easily glance at it in the process of making eye contact with a client. Another option is to use your mobile phone timer to emit a gentle sound when there are 10 minutes left in the session and let the client know that you are doing this to help them finish on time so the client can be on time for other responsibilities or events to which he or she needs to attend.

There is no reason for clinical interviewers to feel uncomfortable about tracking the time in the session. One way to address this is to share a structure with your client for how long the session will last. For example, the practitioner could initiate sessions by saying something like the following: "As usual, we have 1 hour to meet today, and I want to make sure we get to talk about what is on your mind. I will keep track of time so I can let you know when we are near the end of the session, so we have time to talk about how the session went today and make plans for next time." A statement such as this sets the expectation that the session will end on time, that you will track the time, and that you want to hear the client's evaluation of the session. Then the client will not be surprised when your mobile phone sounds the gentle alarm or you glance at the clock and note, "We have 10 (20) minutes left today; let's begin to close the session."

Beginning to end the session when there are 15 or 20 minutes left allows the practitioner to ask if there is a topic that the client wants to talk about that they have not addressed during the session. This strategy can help to avoid clients bringing up important topics at the last minute or what some clinicians label as *door knob communications*. Sometimes, however, clients do have their hand on the office door knob when they share some important detail, such as "By the way, I decided to divorce my spouse." Last-minute communications such as this are often of clinical import, and the last-minute sharing has clinical implications for the client's level of comfort with the topic itself or with the practitioner. If this happens, be empathetic but firm that the session is completed and that you will talk about this at the beginning of the next session, or, if possible, schedule another session sooner than planned. Two role-play examples of handling last-minute issues in session can be found in the following link: https://www.youtube.com/watch?v=n17O4_Uy6Vk.

Bring Closure to Topics That Are Already on the Table

When the session is about 10 minutes from closure, use summarizing statements to review the work and topics that were addressed. This is also a time to point out strengths and find a message of hope, even if it is as basic as noting the courage that the client has in talking about tough issues that day and that this suggests that the client has the strength to work toward resolving his or her concerns. The use of closed questions is also a good strategy for beginning to close the session. However, ask closed questions carefully because even a closed question can call up something new for the client to address, and it does not help to end the session if the practitioner invites the client to share new material when there is only 5 minutes left in the session.

Another approach for using the final 10 minutes of a session is to discuss what might be helpful for the client to think about between now and the next meeting. Depending on the intervention, this might be a time when homework is suggested. For example, cognitive-behavioral interventions often use homework assignments as part of the change process. The solution-focused approach might engage the client in talking about what one small step he or she will take toward the larger solution arrived at in the session that day. Asking clients to suggest some tasks they might do before the next session sends the message that they are the only ones who can create change in their lives and puts them in the power seat.

Evaluate How the Session Was for the Client

The last 10 minutes of a session also includes an evaluation from the perspective of the client. For example, some practitioners ask clients what they want to remember from the session that day. Another way to approach this is to ask clients to share something that went well that day and something that could have been different.

Evaluating the session can also include rehearsal of concrete steps a client might take between sessions because this provides the practitioner with a sense of how much the client took in from an intervention such as an empty chair dialogue. The practitioner could invite clients to role-play what they might say to themselves, for example, when a troubling internal dialogue comes up for them in between sessions. Similarly, clients could be engaged in role-playing how they will react to issues that were addressed in an empty chair strategy that addressed an external dialogue. These role plays also help to evaluate the session from the client's perspective because the activity may provide a concrete example of what the client learned in the session that day; or, if the client stumbles a lot during the role play, it may suggest extra learning to be addressed in the next session.

Reflection on How the Session Was for the Practitioner

Make the time for reflection on how you, as the practitioner, evaluate each session with a client. Ponder the following items:

- What would you do differently next time?
- What new factor did you learn about this client?
- What role did your social identities play in the session?
- Were there any microaggressive moments either from you directed at the client or from the client directed at you? If so, how will you bring this up in supervision and in the next session with the client?
- Were there any moments in which you felt overwhelmed by the client's story; if so, what were they? How will you use supervision to address these moments?
- Reflect on at least one strength you, as the practitioner, brought to the session.

Skills Practice—Closing a Single Session

- Return to working with the same classmate or colleague with whom you took turns to create the audiovisual recording of you interviewing each other to use solution-focused skills or the empty chair strategy to work on a current dilemma in your life (see Chapter 6). Watch the recording again and use it to launch the closing of a single session, which you will also record. As with the initial interview you created in Chapter 6, be your real selves. Do not make up a therapy problem or setting.

- During this interview allow for a break in the role play to examine how your ending of a single session is progressing. This is something that cannot be done in a real session, so take advantage of working with a classmate or colleague to brainstorm ways to successfully close the session.

CLOSING THE ENTIRE CLINICAL RELATIONSHIP

Closing the entire clinical relationship is commonly referred to as termination. Not all terminations are planned endings for various reasons, such as clients not returning for unknown reasons. However, termination can be planned when a client has met his or her goals or insurance coverage dictates the end of the clinical relationship. Although insurance dictates are typically inconvenient for therapeutic processes, they do allow the practitioner and client to know ahead of time how often and for how long they can meet. When the number of sessions is not dictated by insurance coverage, then the practitioner and client use the goals as a guideline for when to end the clinical relationship.

Plan Ahead

When possible, planning ahead for the process of termination is what happens in the best world. The ending process begins with noting how many sessions are left. In cases where insurance dictates the number of sessions, then the practitioner can bring this up: "Today is our fourth session and your insurance allows us to meet eight times, so we are halfway through." When a review of the client's goals suggests that he or she is ready to finish, then the practitioner talks with the client about how many more sessions seem appropriate. For example, after reviewing process on goals, the practitioner might say, "Look at how much you have accomplished; we might be getting close to you not needing to come sessions anymore. I am wondering what you think of having [some number of sessions that fits the work left to be done] sessions before we end?" Choosing the number of sessions still needed is a collaborative endeavor between the client and practitioner and depends on the review the client's completion of goals. This is one of the reasons it helps to create goals that are measureable and concrete, as discussed in Chapter 5.

When termination is planned, the client and practitioner collaborate to choose the number of sessions left. However, starting to count down when there are more than four sessions left is not advisable and, for some clients, counting down from two sessions until goodbye is plenty. The number of sessions may depend on how often the sessions occur—if they are weekly, then four sessions allows for a month to prepare for goodbye and that is plenty; if the sessions are every other week, then four sessions would draw that ending out for too long. Sometimes, the client and practitioner agree to start termination by spacing out the sessions, such as transitioning from one session per week to meeting every other week and then once a month until termination.

Once the number of sessions till termination is decided, then the practitioner reminds the client each week of how many sessions are left. This is not done in a threatening or challenging way, but in a celebratory manner. For example, the practitioner may choose to start or finish each session by noting one of the gains that the client has made: "When I reflect on how many changes you've made, it makes sense that we have two sessions left." Or "Remember how you would have handled that when we first started meeting. It is wonderful to see you have made so much progress; no wonder we will be ending in another week."

Explore Goodbye

Be aware that termination can stir up old, unresolved endings. This is especially true when clients have had many losses in their life or other unplanned goodbyes, such as a client who was in foster care and often moved from home to home without notice. Even when clients do not have unresolved losses or goodbyes, it is imperative that the practitioner address what ending is like for the client. Some clients, especially if they have worked with the practitioner for a long time over months or even a year, may experience a mourning process in which they act angrily toward the practitioner or toward counseling in general. They may act in ways that were problematic when they first started counseling as a way to suggest that they are really not ready to end the clinical relationship. However, many clients will be happy to celebrate the ending and gain back the time they spend in session with the practitioner for other things in their life. It can be helpful for the clinician to talk with the client about how he or she will spend the time that was reserved for counseling as newly found time.

Evaluate and Plan for the Future

The termination process also includes evaluation of the work that was done. Practitioners can introduce this by asking clients about what they learned in the process and how they will practice what they learned over time. Clinicians can also share what they have learned during the process. For example, this can be a way for the clinician to acknowledge elements of the relationship with the client that were positive and those that were challenging. This invites the client to share his or her critique of the practitioner.

The termination phase also includes talking with the client about identifying support systems and how those will be helpful for maintaining changes. Some clients will also benefit from planning for how they will handle things if some of the issues that brought them to counseling resurface. Reviewing the coping skills or other strategies that the client learned to meet his or her goals can build readiness to terminate and confidence in meeting challenges without access to the practitioner. Some clients will also benefit from talking about how they will know or decide if they need future counseling. This is especially true for clients whose issues were related to potentially chronic concerns.

Skills Practice—Termination

- If you have completed all audiovisual recorded skills practices in the preceding chapters and worked with the same classmate or colleague, then you have a series of recordings that cover a number of role-played sessions. Rewatch each of these recordings all in one sitting. Then make notes to yourself on how you would introduce the termination phase to this classmate or colleague. After you have an idea of this from your planning, work with that same classmate or colleague to initiate the termination phase by using each of the steps outlined earlier.
- During this interview allow for a break in the role play and examine how your ending of a single session is progressing. This is something that cannot be done in a real session, so take advantage of working with a classmate or colleague to brainstorm ways to successfully close the session.

WELLNESS EXERCISE

The final wellness exercise offered in this book focuses on gratitude. Research has demonstrated that cultivating gratitude is associated with health and well-being (Emmons & McCullough, 2003; Sansone & Sansone, 2010). For example, Emmons and McCullough (2003) found that making a weekly gratitude list was associated with a more positive outlook on life as well as with being more likely to offer assistance to another person among undergraduate students (Emmons & McCullough, 2003). In another study, Emmons and McCullough (2003) engaged adult participants with an average age of 49 years who had neuromuscular disorders in completing the weekly gratitude list and found that these were associated with higher rates of optimism, higher quality sleep, and a stronger sense of belonging. In light of this evidence, I offer the prompt that the participants in these studies responded to on a weekly basis for a period of 10 weeks to practitioners who are reading this book: "There are many things in our lives, both large and small, that we might be grateful about. Think back over the past week and write down on the lines below up to five things in your life that you are grateful or thankful for" (Emmons & McCullough, 2003, p. 379).

In addition to the weekly gratitude listing, other practitioners may want to practice some of the gratitude exercises suggested by the Harvard Medical School mental health letter (http://www.health.harvard.edu/newsletter_article/in-praise-of-gratitude), such as writing thank you and/or appreciation letters to people who have influenced your life. Imagine thanking someone in your life by sending out wishes of appreciation to someone who has had a positive impact on you. Practitioners who pray can develop a prayer practice that cultivates gratitude, and helping professionals who enjoy mindfulness meditation can find numerous guided gratitude meditations by searching their Web browser with the words "gratitude meditation" and/or by using the script below which can also be found at the following link: http://stillmind.org/gratitude-meditation/.

1. Settle yourself in a relaxed posture. Take a few deep, calming breaths to relax and center. Let your awareness move to your immediate environment: all the things you can smell, taste, touch, see, hear. *Say to yourself: "For this, I am grateful."*

2. Next, bring to mind those people in your life to whom you are close: your friends, family, partner. . . . *Say to yourself, "For this, I am grateful."*

3. Next, turn your attention onto yourself: you are a unique individual, blessed with imagination, the ability to communicate, to learn from the past and plan for the future, to overcome any pain you may be experiencing. *Say to yourself: "For this, I am grateful."*

4. Finally, rest into the realization that life is a precious gift. That you have been born into a period of immense prosperity, that you have the gift of health, culture, and access to spiritual teachings. *Say to yourself: "For this, I am grateful."*

Other mindfulness meditation exercises can be found at the University of California, Los Angeles Mindful Awareness Research Center by using the link http://marc.ucla.edu/mindful-meditations, which has meditations in English and Spanish. The book *Peace Is Every Step* by Thich Nhat Hanh (1992) is also an excellent source for cultivating mindfulness practices for everyday life.

CLOSING COMMENTS

This book introduced you to essential clinical interviewing skills with a social justice and wellness approach. Each chapter challenged you to try out these skills in practice exercises on your own and with a classmate or colleague. Many people who are drawn to professions that require clinical interviewing skills have strong listening skills and a great capacity for empathy. These natural or developed capacities serve them well. However, no one is born or becomes a proficient and successful clinical interviewer without practice, patience, and perseverance. There is no replacement for the lessons learned from creating audiovisual recordings of practicing role-plays with classmates or colleagues and then watching them and getting constructive feedback from the interviewee. When possible and with the proper informed consent, audiovisual recordings of actual work with clients is also an important learning step to be used in clinical supervision with an experienced clinician.

REFERENCES

Emmons, R., & McCullough, M. (2003). Counting blessings versus burdens: An experimental investigation of gratitude and subjective well-being in daily life. *Journal of Personality and Social Psychology, 84*(2), 377–389.

Sansone, R., & Sansone, L. (2010). Gratitude and well-being: The benefits of appreciation. *Psychiatry, 7*(11), 18–22. Retrieved from https://www.ncbi.nlm.nih.gov/pmc/articles/PMC3010965/pdf/PE_7_11_18.pdf

Vajragupta, V. (2007). *Buddhism: Tools for living your life.* Birmingham, UK: Windhorse Publications.

INDEX